PLATE I *The Master*

Charity, Penance, Sacrifice, Duty, Yoga, Devotion, the Expanse of Consciousness, the Substance, Peace, the Truth, Grace, Silence, the supreme State, the deathless Death, Knowledge, Renunciation, Liberation and Bliss, know that all these are synonymous with the severance of the 'body-am-I' Consciousness.

From Maharshi's TRUTH REVEALED

In Days of
Great Peace

THE HIGHEST YOGA AS LIVED

MOUNI SADHU

FOREWORD BY
M. HAFIZ SYED
M.A., PH.D., D.LITT.

1977 EDITION

Published by
Melvin Powers
WILSHIRE BOOK COMPANY
12015 Sherman Road
No. Hollywood, California 91605
Telephone: (213) 875-1711

FIRST PUBLISHED IN 1952

SECOND EDITION REVISED AND ENLARGED
(AND FIRST PUBLISHED BY GEORGE ALLEN AND UNWIN)
IN 1957, REPRINTED 1965, 1970

PUBLISHED IN GERMAN IN 1955
AS AUF DEM PFAD SRI RAMANA MAHARSHIS'

PUBLISHED IN PORTUGUESE IN 1956
AS 'DIAS DE GRANDE PAZ'

Printed by

HAL LEIGHTON PRINTING CO.
P.O. Box 1231
Beverly Hills, California 90213
Telephone: (213) 983-1105

ISBN 0-87980-276-6

Printed in the United States of America

FOREWORD

'Pursue the enquiry "Who am I" relentlessly. Analyse your entire personality. Try to find out where the I-thought begins. Go on with your meditations. Keep turning your attention within. One day the wheel of thought will slow down and an intuition will mysteriously arise. Follow that intuition, let your thinking stop, and it will eventually lead you to the goal'.

From *Maharshi's Teachings*

'If the Supreme Truth is unknown, the study of Scriptures is fruitless; and when the Supreme Truth is realized the study of Scriptures becomes useless'.

From *Sri Sankaracharya*

Most of the people in this world have no faith in spiritual values. To them the human mind is all in all, and this leads them to a variety of reflections and speculations. Some of them call themselves sceptics, others agnostics and yet others pride themselves on being pure materialists. The truth is veiled by our own ignorance. We do not carry our search after it far enough.

Having exercised our intellect up to a certain limit we feel there is no hope for further discovery or investigation. This attitude of the mind is the result of the study of Western systems of philosophy which, from the Eastern point of view, is barren, and leads us nowhere, beyond speculations and guesses at truth.

Whereas Eastern philosophy, more especially Indian system of thought, affords some genuine hope for an earnest aspirant on the path of search for truth. Almost all the ancient thinkers, saints and sages have pointed out an unfailing practical path by pursuing which, one may free oneself of all doubts and uncertainties and realize the meaning and purpose of life. Their method of approach to truth is fairly scientific. They do not dogmatize nor play upon the credulity of our faith. They simply point out a path and lay down certain definite conditions for attaining it.

The final success on this path depends entirely on the aspirant's own effort and self-investigation. The first obvious condition is earnest desire, unquenchable thirst to drink the water of life. In answer to a question as to what are the requisite qualifications of a disciple, Sri Ramana Maharhsi once stated:

'He should have an intense and incessant longing to get free from the miseries of life and to attain supreme, spiritual Bliss. He should not have the least desire for anything else'.

The second is a ceaseless effort with careful and close observance of rules of conduct and the cultivation of the virtues of dispassion and discrimination. The third is the search for a Sad Guru, a genuine teacher who may rightly and successfully guide the aspirant to his destined goal.

It may be added that the ancient Hindu scriptures and the Upanishads have already given us necessary directions as to the path and its achievements. But the truth that is to be found by this definite scientific method is eternal, as acknowledged by the ancient sages, and needs to be testified to by living witnesses from time to time.

It is these sages who have taught us the reasonable assumption and the logical conclusion that only a living teacher can teach us the Upanishadic truth, not the Upanishads themselves, because they are just words and little more, while the living teacher is an incarnation of the truth we seek.

Mouni Sadhu, the writer of the book *In Days of Great Peace*, published in its non-English editions under the title *On the Path of Sri Ramana Maharshi*, seems to have fulfilled all these conditions as far as it is humanly possible. As an earnest seeker he pursued several methods of God realization as taught by various schools of Yoga, occultism and mysticism and finally came to his supreme Master and Guru, Bhagavan Sri Ramana Maharshi who, finding him well equipped with the necessary qualifications enumerated above, granted him His Grace, eradicated his ego-sense (as reported by the author himself) and finally helped and guided him to discover his own eternal and ever-abiding Self.

From our point of view there are two kinds of rational faith in the reality of spiritual life.

1. An indirect faith which we have to have from the experiences and verdicts of such dauntless seekers after truth as had the courage, endurance and iron will to struggle through the thorny path of self-realization and whose words, according to their antecedent and personal integrity, have to be trusted.

2. Faith drawn from direct experience—a thing which no one can possibly doubt or deny.

Mouni Sadhu's book serves as a precious evidence of indirect faith which we have closely and correctly to investigate and ascertain for ourselves. The careful and punctilious author has committed his inexpressible inner experiences to writing as faithfully, accurately and humanly as possible. It is left to us now to make use of it, to the limit of which we are capable.

Actuated by the sense of selfless service and his desire to share with others his experiences and convictions, as a result of his direct knowledge, he has embodied his thoughts and feelings in the form of this fascinating, altogether inspiring and highly instructive book. The earnest readers will find in its perusal not only evidence of one who has crossed the shore of illusory Samsara but enough food for thought and inspiration.

DR. M. HAFIZ SYED

June, 1953

PLATE II *A group of inmates of the Ramanashram*

INTRODUCTION
TO SECOND EDITION

The first edition of this book was published in October, 1952 under the title *In Days of Great Peace . . . Diary Leaves from India.* Following the advice of numerous friendly opinions and many favourable reviews by experts in India and the West, it has been decided to make the revised version slightly longer by some additional chapters based on my old diary and to change the sub-title.

In expressing my own experiences it has seemed best to use as simple a form as possible, avoiding technicalities and classical Yogic terms, which might tend to confuse the student if he is not acquainted with them. In conveying spiritual matters, it is necessary to avoid overburdening the mind, for it distracts the attention, and the main message is not absorbed.

As well as the words of Sri Maharshi spoken in my presence, I have used quotations from the published teachings of the Sage, which were revised and acknowledged by him. They are:

Self-Realisation. Life and Teachings of Sri Ramana Maharshi by B. V. Narasimha Swami, 3rd. ed., 1936
Maha Yoga by 'Who', 3rd ed., 1947
Maharshi's Gospel, 4th ed., 1946
Five Hymns to Sri Arunachala by Sri Maharshi, 3rd ed., 1946
Spiritual Instruction and *Who Am I ?*, two small books compiled from the teachings of the Sage given in writing to his early disciples between 1900 and 1902.

Since Sri Maharshi passed away from the body on 14th April, 1950, some 'new' interpretations and quotations of his sayings have appeared in books written by former inmates of the Ashram. They may be correct, but I prefer to limit myself to the above-mentioned works approved by the Master himself. I have given the reader an account of what I myself experienced, taking full responsibility for the accuracy of what I have written.

IN DAYS OF GREAT PEACE

The teachings of the Sage, passing through the consciousness of each student, must vary in accordance with each one's development, zeal and practice. The teaching itself is so simple that there cannot be any great variation in its main theme, but individual interpretations can differ on unessential points. The truest interpretation is that which arises in the heart of the pupil under the grace of the Master.

True realization does not come from any mental study of the letter of the teaching, neither is a man drawn to attempt the 'Direct Path' because of the accuracy of any biography of the Rishi.

At the beginning of this century a Western Master said: 'One who leaves this earth spiritually blind, will remain so after death'. That is to say, the fact of leaving the body does not, of itself, bring spiritual enlightenment. Sri Maharshi often emphasized our need to attempt to experience Realization *here* and *now*, and no spiritual Master ever contradicts another: Saints and Yogis realize the urgency of the matter, and do not postpone it to some future, unknown state.

Since Realization is nothing more than the raising of our consciousness to the level of reality-spirit-self, which means transcending the so-called 'normal' consciousness of the brain-mind or ego, there must inevitably occur some forms of superconsciousness or—Samadhi. These ecstatic experiences are necessary before the final perennial, or Sahaja Samadhi, can be attained. In the West, some call these Samadhis 'initiations'.

When Sri Maharshi was asked why he did not pass through these 'initiations' in his life, but almost immediately reached Sahaja Samadhi, he replied that one who has reached the summit —must have passed through all the previous initiations in a past life.

So we may accept the fact that these spiritual experiences are necessary before we can reach the state of the 'Liberated', the Rishi, the Jivan Mukta—or simply, the Master. The terms are synonymous.

So each of us must experience this eventually, but at the lowest level the accounts differ, according to individual differences. But the knowledge that others have known them is in itself encouraging to prospective students of the truth of Self.

And this is the only reason for the appearance of this book. When it is asked 'What gave you these experiences?' the only answer which can be expressed in words is this—'The absolute certainty that the path exists, that the goal can be reached and that the Master alone can lead us to it'.

It was also asked 'What happens to a disciple afterwards, when he is separated from the Master's physical form?'

All I can say is that the connection with the Master is never severed. In a mysterious way he leads his followers for ever. Some found that their progress was faster after he left the body, than when they were able to sit in his physical presence.

The Master blesses the seed which he sows in us, and time does the rest, in accordance with the pupil's worthiness of His Grace.

Here we find the reason for an apparently strange fact, that the Master often sends his pupils out into the world, away from the Ashram, that their progress may be completed outside.

After being raised in the hot-house, the plant must continue to grow in the outer air. But the sun which shines on it is still the same.

I am extending my cordial thanks to Miss Nona D. Lucas of Melbourne and to Mr. Gerald J. Yorke of London, whose invaluable co-operation has helped me to improve the text of the present edition.

MOUNI SADHU

June, 1955

PLATE III *Maharshi's attendants with youths*

INTRODUCTION
TO FIRST EDITION

My visit to one of the last great Rishis (sages) of India—known during these past forty years as Sri Ramana Maharshi—was planned four years ago. But the post-war conditions were not favourable to foreign travel, especially if one had to use sea routes and not the speedy airways.

Yet I reached the Ashram in time. In spite of the serious illness of the Sage—everyone realizing that he would soon have to leave this world in which he had lived for over seventy years—it was as easy to approach him, and even to ask questions as before.

But on the whole, visitors were not so anxious to put questions to the great man as to be in his immediate presence. The teachings of Maharshi have been expounded by himself in several short works and many others have been carefully annotated and published by his disciples. Hence his teachings were available for study and were usually read by people before coming to the Ashram. To hear what they already knew was not the chief desire of those who came from so many different parts of the world.

It was the presence of the holy man that attracted, like an invisible and powerful magnet, those who were fortunate enough to have been shown the way to him by the decrees of providence.

* * *

This diary has been written sporadically. I simply tried to make notes in short hasty sentences on scraps of paper, in many cases neither titling nor even dating them, for time somehow seemed to have ceased to exist in this strange corner of the world. I simply wrote down, without any plan, my spiritual experiences, moods, and states of mind as they came day by day when I was sitting at the feet of Maharshi.

I brought from my previous wanderings 'in search of truth' a good deal of mental ballast in the form of various theories of occultism and fragments of the teachings of other Masters. That is why, when I tried to express in words the new inner and transcendental experiences which I had in the presence of Maharshi, they took, in spite of myself, the shape of certain ready-made mental moulds of ideas and even sentences.

No human words can ever express that which we call Truth, Spirit, or God. Yet those who have trodden the path of search before us have left some traces of their experiences in the sacred scriptures of all the religions of the world. We find in them words of such power and beauty that any attempt to seek better forms for *That* which is formless is vain and futile. The words of the great teachers and guides of humanity are streams of power and light. No wonder that every being who finds himself in the presence of one of them enters, as it were almost unconsciously, into this stream.

Often after meditation in Maharshi's presence, short classical sentences, like spiritual axioms, came spontaneously to my memory. Some of those which were used as 'Mottoes' for my diary, have been made into the sub-titles of chapters in this book, as to me they were so much more significant than mere dates.

* * *

I have not tried to write down any of the 'teachings' of Maharshi, as they can be found in many books. My purpose is to record that which the latter do not yet contain, namely, the real experiences of an average man, who wanted to know for himself what the presence of a great Sage means and what its influence is. I had read so many descriptions by pupils who were clever in classifying the qualities and teachings of their Masters, that I should have known, at least in theory, what may be expected in the presence of one of Them. But all theories, all acquired knowledge, falls into dust when one stands face to face with a perfect man. They become as superfluous as the complicated western dress with its collar and tie in the merciless heat of this part of India.

Among the many pupils of Maharshi, now scattered all over the world, Indians are the most numerous. Why is obvious. For so many years, they have been nearer to the light; they have had the best opportunities of getting into touch with the Sage and of understanding his teachings. Many among them are really advanced. Many have had lofty and important spiritual experiences. But these our brethren—Indian Yogis—do not like to talk, still less to write, about their highest flights; instead they prefer to discuss the paths which guide man to these mystical experiences. They undoubtedly have good reasons for such an attitude. First of all, they believe that anything they could possibly say has already been said by the Master, and that no one can do it better than he. And next, Indians have unlimited confidence in the decrees of the Most High. They firmly believe that His is the full responsibility for His creation. Holding such a view, they do not feel any urge to work for the uplifting and improvement of this world. The Westerner, on the other hand, has an innate urge to share his own discoveries and experiences with others, if he feels that such may be of some use to them. So he writes.

I think that both Indians as well as Westerners are to a certain extent right in their respective points of view; only the tasks and 'missions' of both are different.

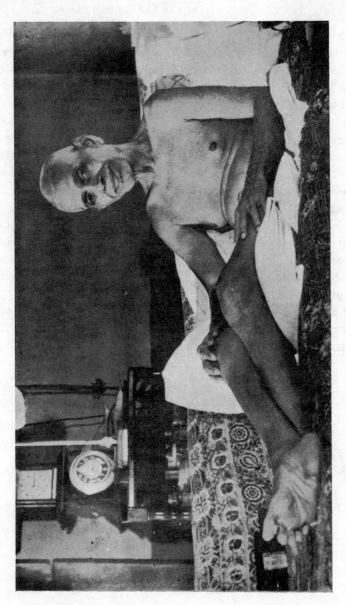

PLATE IV *Maharshi's last months*

CONTENTS

ILLUSTRATIONS

PLATE V   *Mouni Sadhu*

PLATE VI *Entrance to the last abode of Sri Maharshi, his Maha-Nirvana room*

PLATE VII *The Master's Maha-Samadhi*

CHAPTER I

'Association with the Sages...'

'Association with the Sages who have realized the Truth removes material attachments ; on these attachments being removed the attachments of the mind are quite destroyed. Those for whom attachments of the mind are thus destroyed, become one with That which is (ever) motionless. They attain Liberation while yet alive. Cherish (therefore) the association with such Sages'.

From Maharshi's Truth Revealed

Another version :

'Association with the Sages who have realized the Truth cuts off material attachments, on these being dropped, the mental pre-dispositions—due to past Karma and present delusion—are dispelled. Peace in which the unattached ones remain is *That* which is ever unchanging and immovable, it is Jivan Mukti or Liberation here and now. Seek therefore the association with such liberated Beings'.

Ramana Maharshi left this world six months after my departure from India. These words were almost his last :

'They say I am dying. But I shall be here more alive than ever. Where else would I go ?'

Several of his disciples, residing thousands of miles away from the Ashram, knew of his death on the very same day. Comparing the hour with the time when this news was mystically communicated to them, one would say that it was 'broadcast' several hours before Maharshi's body breathed its last.

Letters took a week or more to come from India and elsewhere and they showed that no true disciple of the Master experienced any grief or despair. The same spiritual atmosphere of a lucid wave of peace and light was felt in the hearts of the pupils, whether abroad or in the Ashram of the Saint.

'The world with its physical phenomena is for our Real Self like a dream for the waking man, or like a shadow. Is he concerned with the passing dreams of last night, or with the shadow cast by his body ?'

From *Maharshi's Sayings*

'Not one of the Religions of the world has succeeded in spiritualizing and giving happiness to Humanity. Yet each one has given Liberation—"Salvation", in common language—to many individuals'.

From the Sayings of the famous Indian philosopher Sri Aurobindo.

The spiritual power of every saint and sage is most vividly and directly felt by his contemporaries. With the passing of time what was a revelation becomes only a dead dogma. And when people canonize the saint and build temples to him, they enclose him in their narrow walls, wherein his spirit is suffocated and ceases to be a vivifying and inspiring force. The followers of successive generations quarrel about each and every word ascribed to the Master. They fight for the 'authenticity of texts'. They do all but the one important thing which was taught by the Great One, namely—'to become like unto Him'.

Yet not all the seeds fall on stony ground. Some give a rich harvest. Therein lies hope for the future of erring mankind. The lives of men like Maharshi are the very proofs of this truth. *They are like meteors which in their course brighten the darkest night*.

Those who are able to perceive the path in this flash of light will thenceforward know where it leads.

CHAPTER II

The First Meeting

When I arrived at the abode of Maharshi, called 'Ramanashram' and jumped out from the two-wheeled cart just in front of the temple, in spite of the late hour, but in accordance with the custom of the place, I was taken straight into the presence of the Sage.

He was sitting in a large hall, near one of its walls, apparently at the end of his meal. There were a number of people—all Indians—sitting in rows on the floor between the pillars. I was led to within three or four yards of Maharshi, and my companion said a few words to him of which the name of the country from which I came was the only one I understood. The Saint lifted up his head, looked at me, and made a gesture with his hand as if inviting me to come a little nearer. I was struck by the softness and serenity of this movement, so simple and dignified that I immediately felt I was facing a great man. His attitude was so natural that the newcomer did not feel any wonder or shyness. All his critical faculty of thought and his curiosity dropped away. So I was unable to make observations or comparisons, although subconsciously I may have had this intention when previously imagining this first meeting. The image of the Sage was in this very first moment vividly engraved on my mind, without any qualifications, like a picture cast on a sensitive photo-plate. But as nothing can be conveyed without words, I will try to describe his appearance.

Maharshi, as I saw him, was a thin, white-haired, very gracious old man; his skin had the colour of old ivory; his movements were easy, calm and soft; his countenance breathed a natural state of inner concentration without the slightest effort of will. Or may I say that he had reached that stage when will-power no longer needs to be used for overcoming any hindrance, or for achieving any purpose? For the simple reason that *everything has already been achieved.*

It was the first manifestation of the invisible radiance which I witnessed every day during subsequent months. Just now as I am writing these words, I wonder how it is that I have never forgotten even the smallest detail concerning Maharshi; it can be evoked in my brain like a picture on a hidden sensitive plate of whose very existence I was unaware.

A modest Indian supper was served—a little rice, vegetables and fruit on a banana leaf. By the time I had finished Maharshi had gone. As soon as I found myself in the small one-room cottage prepared for me in the Ashram's compound, I immediately fell asleep, being very tired after my whole day's journey.

CHAPTER III

Life in Maharshi's Ashram

The next day was occupied in getting acquainted with the routine of the Ashram; the hours of meditation in the presence of the Sage; the time of meals in the dining-hall, and so on.

I had to protect some foodstuffs, which I had brought with me, against the ants. They quickly found their way to my sugar and biscuits and gathered round my tins of honey, although these were hermetically sealed. I had also to arrange for drinking-water to be brought from the nearby tap.

The simple way of life in the Ashram helps one to concentrate and dive deep into oneself; the very atmosphere, charged with the thoughts of so many people seeking their real Self, according to the teachings of the Master, turns the mind inwards and is favourable to introspection. The invisible yet powerful influence of the sacred hill of Arunachala also has its part in creating this peculiar atmosphere, but of that I will speak later.

At 7 a.m. there was the loud sound of a gong calling us to breakfast. When I reached the dining-hall, Maharshi was just mounting the few steps leading to it. He was accompanied by several Indians, his permanent attendants. Here, in full daylight, I noticed for the first time, that the physical state of Maharshi was really precarious. He walked with difficulty, as his joints and knees were affected by acute rheumatism. His left arm and elbow were bandaged because of a malignant tumour, which had begun its growth about six months earlier and, in spite of two operations, had continued to spread its devastating work, causing Maharshi's death one year later. Sometimes his head shook slightly and this increased the impression of serious ill-health; the whole frame, once tall and powerful, was now bent and weak.

After reaching the hall, Maharshi took his place near the wall, opposite the entrance. He sat alone, while facing him plantain leaves were spread on the floor for the rest of the residents. I occupied a place on his right, about three yards away, and that spot remained mine during the whole period of my stay.

The Sage ate with his hand according to the general Indian custom. His movements seemed to be automatic. I saw that he was quite aware of his surroundings and reacted in a normal way to all the phenomena of the outward world, but I felt certain that his real Self had nothing to do with the functions and actions of his visible vehicle. After some time I understood that, according to his own teachings, this physical plane of existence was like a dream for him. I also understood that unless I were able to realize for myself this state as regards the outer world, I could never know reality.

The grasping of this truth is our first real step to getting rid of the mind's fetters. During all our lives, the mind constantly creates scores of purposeless thoughts. One of the European disciples of the Sage rightly remarked:

'Our mind creates its own problems and then tries to solve them, but it will never find a final solution, as this does not exist in its limited sphere of activity'.

There are three communal meals in the Ashram : lunch or dinner at about 11.30 a.m., supper at 7.30 p.m. and also tea at 3.30 p.m. for the Ashram guests and occasional visitors. One is given tea, coffee, or by special request milk, as was the case with me. The dishes are well prepared, but some vegetables and pastry have many condiments added and are too hot for the European palate. But I soon discovered that in this tropical climate the stronger spices are good and I took all the burning curries and sauces, with only a few exceptions, though I must admit that the Brahmins who served us, after noticing what remained on my plantain leaf, ceased serving me the hottest dishes.

Maharshi took a little of everything. At the end of the meal, when buttermilk was distributed, he made a kind of round wall of rice, leaving a space in the middle for the liquid. When he had enough he stopped with a gesture the Brahmin who was serving.

He never left a single grain of rice on his leaf. This is regarded as a
duty by everyone obeying Hindu customs, which direct each step
the individual takes on the physical plane. In the beginning I could
not understand this seeming submission to outer customs by a
great Sage who sees the whole world as an illusion of the mind and
its servants, the five senses. But later on, when in the presence of
Maharshi, my own mind became more and more quiet, more fit
to judge rightly, and when all the horizons of thought were
clearer, this doubt, as well as many others, disappeared.

During the first weeks of my stay in the Ashram, Maharshi
spent the whole day, with the exception of the hours of sleep and
food, under a small bamboo roof near the library building, facing
the dining hall. He reclined on a big stone couch covered with
mats, cotton rugs and a few pillows.

As soon as I saw the stone couch, the thought came to my mind,
which according to the old European habit must judge everything
by its appearance, that Maharshi's rheumatism may have developed
from sitting for many years on stone. I did not realize that what
may be true in colder countries need not necessarily be so in India,
for afterwards I found, during my night wanderings on the sacred
Hill Arunachala, that the big rocks where I sat were quite warm
several hours after sunset, and did not become cold the whole
night through.

His disciples and visitors sat on the concrete floor facing Maharshi.
For the morning and evening meditations certain Sadhus, pupils
of the Master, often came from the caves of Arunachala. Every
day the Vedas were recited and before the night meal holy hymns
were chanted, often those composed by Maharshi himself in his
younger days. Every fortnight one of the permanent residents, a
learned Brahmin, sang a most beautiful hymn; it was, as I learned,
in praise of the 'Lord of the Universe'. It was full of melodic impli-
cations and the endings of the words, which, of course, I did not
understand, will forever remain in my memory, like so many
other things in this abode of peace.

Later, amidst the turmoil of worldly life, when I remembered

Maharshi's words: '*Think about your real Self*' and understood the need of doing so, I found that the memory of this melody, the sound of it inwardly heard, immediately established harmony in my consciousness.

It took some time before I could adjust myself to the rhythm of the Ashram life and could inwardly approach Maharshi. At first I had to struggle with mental distrust, with the tendency to look for blemishes in the lives of those who surrounded the Sage. I was simply wasting precious time in a vain fight with my mental windmills. I was looking on Maharshi from the narrow citadel of the ego, of my own small personality. I was aware that I should not do so, that I should step out of my self into a broader path, and that only thus could I find enlightenment.

I was going through a trial well known to occult psychologists. The mind may reason and discuss lofty matters, it may even be able to create works where spiritual ideas are well expounded under the inspiration of the Master. But when the real, the actual experience approaches, when one has to *live* what was so cleverly expressed, ah! then a gap appears, a jarring note sounds.

Yet as days passed, the radiance emanating from the Sage was slowly doing its invisible work. At first I wanted to have a talk with him, but I was disheartened by the shallowness of what I tried to say. Then at last, intuition showed the proper way:

'Silence is the most powerful form of teaching transmitted from Master to pupil. There is no word by which one can convey the important things, the deepest truths'.

From *Maharshi's Sayings*

I began to listen intently to the silence surrounding the Master. I understood what a high degree of concentration, of the control of the movement of thoughts, is necessary to be able to open the door of the mind to the subtle vibrations constantly radiated by Maharshi and leading one to high initiation. I also came to understand that my previous exercises were not of the best; that here they would prove insufficient. At first it was rather depressing to see that all my former methods had to be re-examined and changed.

I realized that the amount of knowledge I could find and assimilate here depended upon my own attitude and that I myself was responsible for catching and using to the full this unique opportunity of being at Maharshi's feet, an opportunity which would never again be repeated. In other words, the amount of light penetrating into my being would depend directly upon the opening of the doors of my consciousness.

In practice it was not at all easy to let go all my self-centred opinions, all forms of crystallized beliefs, comparisons and prejudices. Many of these beliefs had been regarded by me as unshakable and now I saw that they would not stand the fiery test of the presence of one who had realized the truth. Comparison with some Masters of the past was especially responsible for many moments of inner conflict. What, I queried, is the role of Buddha, of Christ and of other great Masters who have shown Humanity such wonderful paths to salvation? Should we not adhere to those who have given us such unmistakable signs of their divinity? Should we not continue to walk in their holy footsteps?

There were many other doubts and hesitations, but I do not think it useful to repeat here all such misconceived ideas. The answers to my doubts came quite unexpectedly and simply as did everything in this strange abode. I was told that once, when a European Roman Catholic couple were sitting at Maharshi's feet, and probably under the charm of the incomparable sanctity and sublimity of the atmosphere, were expressing their emotions in the form of prayers traditionally most familiar to them, the Sage remarked:

'They have another Master. They pray to him. But this makes no difference. There is but *One*'.

I had read much about Maharshi before coming to the Ashram. I knew that he sees the content of the inner being of every man who approaches him, although he never shows that he does so, or speaks about it. So this case was not surprising to me. But I had also personally to experience this extraordinary power of the Master. It was essential, for without a complete trust in the Master, without a belief that his consciousness is one with the Absolute, as well as one with that of his pupil, the realization of self-knowledge is impossible.

As week after week is spent near him, the shell of the separated personality bursts and dissolves. I always feel this process when I am with him. The important turning-point in my own life came on the day when Maharshi had moved, according to the decision of the Ashram 'high command' (his brother and the staff administering the outer affairs of the Ashram) to the hall of the newly-built temple. It was built in purely Hindu style on the spot where his mother was buried in 1922. There were rumours that at first, Maharshi did not want to move, saying he was quite comfortable under the little bamboo roof. But when his brother, the Superintendent of the Ashram and some of his staff, prostrated before the Saint, imploring him to agree, he answered that it mattered little where one stays and yielded to their entreaties.

A big couch carved in granite and covered with embroidered Indian rugs was awaiting the Sage in the hall of the temple which was to be his last abode.

The temple, in the ancient traditional Hindu style with the happy addition of some modern comforts, is built from grey granite, which has been beautifully carved. With not too many sculptures or other ornamentation, with slender columns in the middle, large windows and many doors, with modern electric fans and strong fluorescent lamps, it makes a very pleasant impression indeed. Near Maharshi's couch stood a shelf with books, a small table and a clock, and in front of him was an incense-holder, with Indian incense sticks burning all day long, and spreading their fragrance throughout the hall.

At noon Maharshi was taken into the temple-hall with some solemnity, but I was not present, as I had left after the morning meditation. When I returned in the afternoon, I had to find a place for myself in this new abode, and chose one by the nearest column facing Maharshi, from which I could always look into his eyes.

The hall was divided into two parts. Men sat on the right side and women on the left. A small portable barrier in front of the Sage's couch, showed the limit of approach to the devotees and visitors.

Maharshi was sitting as usual, with legs crossed in a posture of meditation and reclining on several pillows, his head slightly bent towards the shoulder. One could see that the previous ceremonies had tired his weak physical frame. This weakness troubled me at first, if one can be troubled at all in his presence. Later on I became accustomed to this sight. I also came to pay less attention to the 'visible' side of things and therefore was less anxious or concerned about it.

The recitation of the Vedas began about 5.15 p.m. and lasted for forty-five minutes. After that Maharshi went through his letters, which came from all parts of the world, gave a hasty glance at the newspapers, and then the secretary of the Ashram, an educated Indian with a long grayish beard, a loin cloth and a piece of white towelling over his shoulders as his only garments, brought a pile of letters for approval in answer to the previous day's mail. Maharshi carefully read them all, putting them back into their respective addressed envelopes. Sometimes the Sage made a few remarks, but this was rather rare and then the secretary took back such letters for correction in accordance with his suggestions.

At last all the activities of the day came to an end and there was silence and peace.

CHAPTER IV

Tears

With some effort of will I impose calm on my mind. It does not create thoughts any more. Those which appear immediately vanish like small clouds in the Indian sky. I am gazing intently at the Saint, looking into his great widely-opened dark eyes.

And suddenly I begin to *understand*. How can I express in our earthly language what exactly I do understand? How shall I tell in words, based on the common ideas and experiences of ordinary people who are creating and moulding our language, these higher and more subtle things? May I say that I understand that Maharshi's life is not concentrated on this our earthly plane; that it extends far beyond our world; that he contemplates a different and real world, a world not subject to storms and changes; that he is a torch of *light* before the throne of the Most High, shedding its rays all round; that he is like the incense smoke constantly rising towards the blue sky which we see through the temple roof; that his eyes, just now looking at me, seem to convey—no, I am unable to say anything more, I cannot even think.

I only feel a stream of tears upon my face. They are abundant and serene. They flow silently. It is not suffering, regret, or repentance that is their source. I do not know how to name their cause. And through these tears I look at the Master. He knows full well their origin. His serious, almost solemn face, expresses endless understanding and friendship and glows with *inner light* which makes it so different from all other human faces. In the light of his profound gaze I suddenly understand the reason and purpose of my tears. Yes, I 'see' at last. The sudden illumination is too strong to allow immediate belief in the truth of the 'seen'. Is 'this' really possible? Can it be possible? But Maharshi's eyes seem to bring a confirmation of 'it'.

I can only say that there are moments of inner experience so important, so fraught with consequences, that they may influence not only one but many incarnations. There are stains which have to be washed out before more light can be seen. No water from an earthly vessel can wash them out, can purify the soul. It may be that the only vessel which can serve this purpose is the heart, the only 'water' a stream of tears.

'*Peace that passeth all human understanding*'.

Similar meditations continue for a few more days, and are followed by another stage. Tears give way to an inner quietude and a feeling of inexpressible, indescribable happiness. This inner mood is independent of any outward condition. Neither the pain of the limbs, which is often annoying when one has been sitting for several hours in the same position, nor the troublesome, black mosquitoes, nor the trying heat, can disturb this inner peace. This state lasts as long as I do not allow the mind to create new thoughts. But as soon as the concentration ceases, peace also vanishes. And once more the world with its problems steps in, worries, anxieties, expectations, appear again.

But once we have discovered the secret of this experience, the door to its repetition is opened. We can recover it at will. I am quite aware that the assistance of the Master is a most important factor in these first glimpses of the supramental consciousness. I do not think he is definitely and actively intervening, but his *presence*, his constant *radiation* spontaneously brings about this effect.

I look at the people gathered in the temple hall. Brahmins and outcastes, Europeans and Americans, men and women, the old, the young and small children. All are happy here at the feet of the Saint. Everyone feels this happiness according to his own capacity and degree of receptivity.

The learned Brahmin may think that by being here he is nearer to liberation from the wheel of births and deaths. The black Dravidian farmer trusts that the crops on his small rice field will be richer after his visit to the Ashram to pay homage at the feet of the Rishi. An American may hope to find salvation and the bliss of

C

Samadhi : and an artiste, a former film-star from North India, beautiful in her silver-grey sari, may already feel herself to be in 'Svarga', the Hindu paradise.

And to me it seems that the thick mist covering the horizon is slowly becoming less dense, that the day is nearing when nothing will stand any more between me and reality. I also see in these moments the tremendous amount of labour ahead of me. I see that I am short of so many of the necessary qualifications. But this sight does not bring depression as it usually did before. The experienced peace being out of time, the question 'when' and 'how' does not arise.

I remember Maharshi's words in answer to a similar question. I read them lately and they seem to confirm my feeling.

'*The Real Self is all, it is omnipresent, hence always with us. To live in it is Realization*'.

CHAPTER V

'The Glory of the Lord is Manifested in His Saints'

Today I have carefully watched Maharshi when he was 'officiating' or, as the Hindus say—'giving Darshan', which means he is visible for all to see. From morning till noon and from 3.30 p.m. till evening he sits in the temple hall, or under the bamboo roof near the library, surrounded by a group of pupils and residents of the Ashram, and by a crowd of visitors and pilgrims. He speaks very little and cases where he directly addresses anyone are rare indeed.

His face is full of inspiration, unearthly serenity and power, of infinite kindness and understanding. Big dark eyes seem to look into the infinite, above the heads of all present, without appearing to concentrate on anyone in particular, and yet penetrating to the deepest recesses of each individual heart. This can be felt as one looks into them. And it is really difficult not to plunge our gaze into those eyes when we are near Maharshi. He reigns in silence over this varied crowd, being a focus for so many different human feelings.

The ways of our thought are being changed here; new ideas enter the field of our consciousness. The atmosphere of utter purity and peace constantly radiated by the Sage compels each one of us to examine and verify, as it were, all our beliefs and opinions; yet it comes by itself spontaneously, without any effort on our part; it is not imposed, it is simply the result of a sudden enlargement of consciousness. This inner process is accompanied by a sense of great happiness. It is not passivity of the mind, 'dolce far niente' as the Italians say—not at all; this state is our birthright, as it were, earned by a long practice of concentration and purification of the mind from all the rubbish of worldly thoughts. In the presence of Maharshi this process becomes free and *natural*. It ceases to be a labour and a toil, an effort without any certainty of success as it so often is.

I come out for a moment from my meditation to look at the Master. I know that in a second I shall be able to return to it with the greatest ease, plunging again into the same inner world. Maharshi is sitting as before with his head slightly bent over one shoulder, with his immobile gaze fixed in the vast beyond. The electric lights have been switched on, and women, who have to leave the hall at 6 p.m., have already left. Only about a dozen people remain who every night take part in the most mystic, invisible 'worship' performed by Maharshi at this hour of the day. This word 'worship' may not be either a strict or an adequate expression, but for a moment, I cannot find a better one, and I do not want to seek for words laboriously; the sensitive reader will understand, and to those who are unable to grasp these things, even the most suitable words will be of no avail.

I suddenly realize that these are the *last* months of Maharshi's service to humanity in this, his human form. The days of his life in this body may be really few, in spite of the fact that some of his devotees are still hoping for a miracle. I hear there will be one more operation. Personally, I am unable to await any 'miracle'. The glow, the reflection, of the real which I see through the Master illumines the mind. It sees more clearly now and perhaps is nearer to truth.

If anything happens according to the highest will of *That* which establishes the laws of existence, out of which we are able to see only effects, it would be senseless to hope for that same will to contradict itself. If the last sacrifice of the Saint has taken the form of an incurable disease, according to laws known to us, which always lead in an appropriate time to the death of the physical body, how then can it happen that His will be resisted? It would be a contradiction, impossible to admit, even for the limited human mind.

Hence I personally have no consolation in this hope for a 'miracle'. But I have another one, namely, that I do not believe at all in the 'departure' of the Master. Although I have not by any means yet won my last battle with Matter, or rather with its illusion, and probably my way to this victory is still long, I already *do not believe* in the real existence of the enemy. If he were real there could be no path, no possibility of victory at all, as—*the real cannot be overthrown.*

For me Maharshi *will never depart.* It was not without a definite purpose, that it has been given to us, who are now surrounding the Sage, to be born in the same time with him and to have the privilege of seeing the light he sheds upon the world, I remember his own words spoken to a pupil on this matter.

A wave of endless bliss surges through and overwhelms me. It carries me beyond thought, beyond suffering and grief; neither death nor change exist there, only infinite *being.* Time disappears —there is no need of it any more.

I do not know how long this wave of *light* reigned within me. At last I felt I should look—through my closed eyelids—at the Master. And—without opening my eyes—I 'see' or rather *know* that the Saint has fixed his immovable gaze upon me.

That is the key to my experience.

CHAPTER VI

The Man Sri Maharshi

Maharshi was born on 31st December, 1879, in a village near
Madura in South India. He was named Venkataraman; he belonged to a respected but not affluent Brahmin family, his father
being a pleader. He and his elder brother were educated at the
local High School; at sixteen he was preparing for matriculation
at Madras University. Up to that time there was nothing to make
anyone suspect that a spiritual genius was here in embryo. Venkataraman was a beautiful healthy boy, loving sport and physical
exercise, but not over keen on study. There was a legend in his
family that, from every generation, one of its sons would leave
home and discard the worldly life. The only spiritual books which
had made an impression on the boy were the *Life of Kabir*, and
descriptions of the lives of sixty-three Saints of Shiva's cult.
Maharshi later said that when he read the latter, a strange desire
arose in him, a yearning to be one of those Saints. Finally, when
listening to his uncle speaking about pilgrimage to Arunachala, a
holy hill some hundred miles from Madura, the very word
'Arunachala' struck a responsive chord in the heart of the youth.
He asked his uncle to tell him about this Mount Arunachala.

Some time later, he had an extraordinary experience. Suddenly,
while alone in his room, a terrible fear and realization of death
overcame him. The young Venkataraman, in perfect health and
without any outward suffering, felt that his last hour had come.
His reaction was entirely different from what one would expect.
He called for no help, nor did he seek a doctor, but quietly lay
down on the floor, saying to himself: 'Death is coming to me, but
death of *what*. My body is already lying without movement, it is
becoming cold and stiff, but "I", my consciousness, is not affected
at all. "I" am therefore independent of this dying form. "I" am
not this body'. After some time life came back to the corpse-like

body, but its dweller was changed. His experience brought to him the conviction of the independence of his real Self from the temporary form falsely called 'I'.

Shortly after this he left Madura, giving no indication of his destination, leaving only a note for his family asking them not to worry and not to seek him, as he assured them he was embarking on a virtuous enterprise. Taking only enough money to pay part of his fare, he travelled by train and on foot to Tiruvannamalai, the nearest township to Mount Arunachala. He then stayed at the numerous temples and shrines in the neighbourhood, cutting his hair and discarding his Brahmin clothes as a sign of his renunciation of the world. Nobody knew him; he sat for days unconscious of his body, immersed in deep Samadhi, and at first, the new spiritual awakening brought complete neglect of his outer personality.

Hungry and emaciated, eating only the scraps of food brought to him by visitors who took pity on the young ascetic, and speaking no word in his observance of the silence (mouna), the future Great Rishi spent long years of extremely strenuous life at the foot of the sacred Arunachala.

The fame of the boy grew. Now food was offered to him in plenty, but he took only what was needed to keep alight the flame of his physical life. His spirituality was such that no one of any perception could come near him without recognizing his unique quality.

Then came the first disciples in the persons of various Swamis and devotees. In those years of complete Silence he left us his first written teachings, addressed to some faithful attendants who wanted to have his instructions. In extremely concentrated form the young Sage gave his teaching to the world in two small books entitled—*Who Am I ?* and *Spiritual Instruction*.

This phase of strictly ascetic life in caves on the sacred hill of Arunachala ended at the repeated entreaties of his attendants, and he took up his abode in a small shelter in a clearing in the jungle at the foot of the hill.

In the meantime his mother and his only living younger brother, the future superintendent of the Ashram, found him and begged him to return home. He refused, but when his mother lost the house where he was born, and had no one to support her ageing years, he agreed to her living at the Ashram. She looked after the cooking for him, his attendants and visitors, and became his pupil. Under his guidance it is believed that she attained Samadhi.

A new period of life began for the Sage. From near and far came pilgrims and devotees who had heard of the unique spirituality of Maharshi. The name was first bestowed on him by a learned pandit—Ganapati Sastri—who sat at his feet, plying him with questions. From the answers given, it was recognized that the young Saint was of the highest rank, known in India as Great Rishis, or 'seers'. After the publication of a book by Narasimha Swami, about the life and teachings of Maharshi, and after *A Search in Secret India* by Paul Brunton appeared in London, an uninterrupted flow of visitors from all over the world began.

Talks with him by pilgrims from all over the country, and his answers to their problems, became famous. Eminent intellectuals from the West also sat at his feet, and some of their reminiscences have appeared in *At the Foot of Arunachala*, published at his fifty years jubilee.

His brother had taken over the management of the Ashram's affairs, administering them with great ability. But Maharshi never cared for temporal and evanescent things. All his earthly possessions were a bamboo stick, a wooden bowl for water (kamandalu) and a loin-cloth.

Besides the previously mentioned two small books, Maharshi wrote some hymns with commentaries, in Sanskrit, Tamil and Telugu. These have been translated into English, some with fore-words by eminent English writers.

Throughout his life the Great Rishi was always accessible to any visitor. In his presence no distinction was given to caste, so rigidly followed in India. Brahmins sat with Pariahs, Moslems and Westerners. The visible presence of the Spirit-in-Man united the troubled world at his feet. He was supreme, far above all levels of human understanding. That intangible atmosphere of spiritual peace dissolved all doubts in his presence.

The writer came to him in the very last period of his earthly life, and believes this to be the most glorious period of all. As the sun sinks in a blaze of sunset glory, so Maharshi's last years reflected the indescribable beauty of his manifestation.

I saw the man, as he showed the victory of spirit over matter. His physical suffering, lasting for more than a year, was a crucifixion in my eyes. For him there was no alleviation in hospital, although his sickness was deadly. He always gave the permanent Darshan—for our sakes. He always sat before us, and no movement or complaint ever showed the depth of his suffering. He took no anaesthetics. He wanted no cure. Knowing all that could be expected of his physical body, his thought was always for us, who went to him to seek relief from our own sufferings, and to none did he refuse his blessing. His spiritual alchemy transmuted the hard materialism of our hearts into something pure and noble.

In the glory of his presence, we learned to live in eternity, to remember our lost inheritance of spirit and bliss. Sometimes when I sat near him absorbing the invisible radiations of His light, I meditated: to whom and when can I repay this bliss? Who is it that is taking away the burdens and debts of my life? He has no sin, has never performed an evil deed. But what is there about me, about all of us who are gathered together at his feet, seeking solace and power to endure our petty discomforts? His body, which has committed no sin, is suffering agony in our presence, who are healthy in spite of our guilt.

The mysterious voice asks: 'Are you ready to accept responsibility for *That*?' The soundless answer is: 'Yes, if you will always be with me'. And the conviction arises within that *he is*, and *will be forever*.

CHAPTER VII

A Wish Fulfilled

Many years ago, under the sky of a far-off country in Europe, in the third year of the terrible conflagration of the First World War, a young man in military uniform was sitting on the platform of a small railway station waiting for his train. It was to take him to the front line, where the fire of battle was then raging, a fire from which so many never returned. Compelled by the storm of war to leave his family and his studies, he sat there brooding over the fate awaiting him in a few days.

It was the beginning of Autumn, a season when the dark night skies are often cut by the fiery lines of 'falling stars', or meteors. He remembered a current belief that 'a wish spontaneously expressed in the very second when such a star falls is always fulfilled.'

Unconsciously, he was looking into the sky with a strange expectation. Suddenly a bright red line appeared among the glowing stars. The heart of the young man whispered the one word—'Love'.

Many years passed. This moment of the 'falling star' vanished completely from his memory. The deep wish of the heart was utterly forgotten in the fever and bustle of worldly life. The young dreamer, now a mature man, went through all the experiences of normal life: he had friends; he loved, as he believed, women; he revered those whom he regarded as his superiors. But each experience brought him a disappointment. At the end of each one he saw that not yet had he found true love, which would give him the fullness that was unconsciously his constant longing. He felt in every 'love' a jarring note, a hidden doubt, a small flaw. Hence he was never able to give to anyone without reservation such a depth of affection and love in the midst of which he could not dream of a still greater and deeper one.

A soundless yet powerful voice was always whispering in his

heart: 'It is not that, nor yet is it this'. But at the same time, in moments of peace, he was certain that somewhere, beyond a stormy sea and a cloudy sky there is a mysterious land, where 'the sun of bliss never sets, where the eternal waves are surging *without movement* on the shores of the Island called *fulfilment*'.

CHAPTER VIII

Love

*'In my unloving self thou didst create a passion for thee, therefore
forsake me not, Oh, Ramana Arunachala!'*
Paraphrase of *Maharshi's Hymn*

Thirty years later in far-off India, a pilgrim was sitting under the
bamboo roof of an Ashram, in the ancient place called Tiruvannamalai. It was the same man who in his youth looked one dark
night into the northern sky, waiting for falling stars, to ask them
about his future fate. Many years had passed. Many conditions of
life had changed, as well as many boundaries of States. Some had
fallen down, while other had been newly created in the tremendous upheaval of the two great wars. Yet, in spite of suffering and
devastation the world had not solved any of its chief problems,
had not understood any of the causes of these two terrible calami-
ties. The nightmare of a new catastrophe was hanging over the
dwellers of this unhappy planet, which according to Hindu sacred
books, is passing through the 'Kali-Yuga' or, the dark period of
deepest immersion in matter.

But nothing of all this was felt in Maharshi's Ashram. An utterly
different atmosphere reigned here—no brutal, coarse, or violent
element of the outer world had any access to it.

The former young dreamer was now sitting at the feet of and
face to face with a being who had solved all human problems. He
was looking back on all the past years of his life, trying to do his
final accounts. He was examining the meaning of his goal, weighing the value of his previous experiences. And new vistas were just
opening before him. The shadows of old attachments and 'loves'
were rapidly passing before his eyes and vanishing forever, being
unable to withstand the fiery test of the silent presence of the
Master. How ridiculous now seemed his former efforts to find a
'harmony' in surroundings where human purposes were so dia-

metrically different from his own; in the midst of clashes of selfish interests and tendencies, and of ruthless attempts to exploit others for his own purpose and pleasure.

The tragic comedy of earthly love now appeared in all its unattractive nakedness before the tribunal of his consciousness.

From the other side, a new vision was entering the temple of his soul, just vacated by the impostors, a luminous ideal, incorruptible, pure, devoid of any stain of selfishness, resplendent with spiritual beauty, and independent of all ephemeral physical forms. Here was no more possibility of disappointment, of friction, and of misunderstanding.

It is only now that the pilgrim understands the meaning of his own wish, whose fulfilment was promised in the springtide of his life, by the falling star. He accepted this promise without reservation, knowing that its realization was the turning point of his life. He saw more clearly that the new path led into the infinite. But now there was no more fear. Infinity is life, and all that is finite is in the realm of death.

*   *   *

Maharshi has a strange power to awaken love for himself in the hearts of all; this devotion uplifts his pupils, incalculably raising the level of their lives, enabling them to touch the purest form of this power-energy that is perhaps the creator of the universe. Love and devotion for the Saint have none of the ugly qualities of an ordinary love, like jealousy, possessiveness, exclusiveness, falling under the spell of outer appearances, uncertainty and delusiveness, and last, but not least, the pain of separation from the object of love. Here the love-devotion for the Master does not ask for anything in return. It asks only for the grace of utterly giving oneself to him, to enter into unity with the perfect and all-pervading object.

One who realizes the true greatness of the Sage understands, that he must discard his personality and henceforth make it no more the basis of his existence. He has to transcend the boundaries of the mental-emotional self, if he wants to achieve union with the object of his love, and these words mean something utterly different from the sense usually attributed to them. He can know the real beauty of the Master only by entering the kingdom of the Master's Self. That which we see of him on the physical plane is a mere shadow of him as he really *is*. But those who have been in his presence know how powerful is even this reflection.

There was one tragic evening in the Ashram. The state of Maharshi's health was suddenly worse and one could notice at first glance a great tiredness in his face and a weakness of the whole body. During the usual recitation of the Vedas his head was helplessly sinking lower and lower, although now and again he tried, with a visible effort, to resume the habitual meditative posture. Just before 6 p.m. when the temple hall was almost empty, except for a small group of his nearest attendants and pupils, we suddenly saw big stains of blood on the bandage enveloping his arm and even on the white pillows supporting it. The young Indian attendants were terrified. One ran to the doctor residing nearby, who was in the habit of dressing the wound every day in the small dispensary of the Ashram.

Dead silence fell on all. Some of the women wept; the faces of the men were serious and deeply worried. But Maharshi himself seemed utterly indifferent to all this. He looked upon his arm with a strange expression as if he were quietly contemplating a thing quite foreign to, or without any connection with, himself. Then with his unique soft gesture, showing the stained pillow almost as if he would like to beg us to excuse him for the trouble, he smiled. That was all. What was felt by the people round him as the icy breath of death, had made no impression on him.

All of us who were then sitting at his feet were united in the same spontaneous impulse, and understood each other perfectly in this tragic moment, without the need of words or even glances. Each one of us would gladly have given all his blood in exchange for that which the Master had lost, if it could only delay the imminent catastrophe.

The doctor came, out of breath; he was a short elderly Indian gentleman, looking somewhat like a Malayan. He began dressing the arm, bidding Maharshi to leave the hall earlier in view of this happening, which was to prove a turn for the worse in his condition. But the Saint refused with his typical kind gesture. He looked on the people gathered round and once more a marvellous smile illumined his face. One would say that he wished to compensate for the grief seen in our hearts, which we were quite certain, were open to his gaze.

I have never seen, and undoubtedly shall never see, on any other face, such an inexpressibly wonderful smile as Maharshi's. A spotless purity, love for all, and a wise understanding of our imperfections and shortcomings, all this and far more, was contained in his smile, something which no words can convey. A transcendent beauty reflected in physical form? Only those who have seen it will understand.

I pondered: such an ocean of love, such a power of adoration directed towards the Sage, could they not have some weight before providence somewhat to delay the tragic happening; tragic of course, only for us.

At that very moment I instinctively lifted up my head. I found the answer deep in the eyes of the Saint, and silence was restored in my heart as I breathed:

'O Lord, just are all thy doings'.

*　　　*　　　*

Today I read a passage which throws much light on the mysterious illness of Maharshi, so incomprehensible to his devotees:

'When the average person suffers for his fellow man, he calls it compassion. A famous contemporary Yogi—Sri Yogananda Paramahamsa, describes it as "metaphysically induced illness". For two years before his death, Yogananda suffered from this type of illness and according to his disciples, it was the result of "working out" in his own body some of the physical and spiritual burdens of his friends and disciples. In his Autobiography, Yogananda explains this phenomenon as follows: "The metaphysical method of physical transfer of disease is known to highly advanced Yogis. A strong man can assist a weaker one by helping to carry his heavy load; a spiritual superman is able to minimize his disciples' physical or mental burdens by sharing the Karma of their past actions. Just as a rich man loses some money when he pays off a large debt for his prodigal son, who is thus saved from the dire consequences of his own folly, so a Master willingly sacrifices a portion of his bodily wealth to lighten the misery of his disciples'.

CHAPTER IX

My Path to Maharshi

It is usually a bad plan to revive the past where it touches one's personality; but in reviewing my present Diary, a question arose: 'Before I met Maharshi, why did I consider all my previous experiences in occultism to be failures?'

At 25 years of age, Theosophy attracted my attention. Its smooth and logical theories pleased my reason, as did the impeccable style of Mrs. Besant and Mr. Leadbeater. For some time I corresponded with both. Then the honesty and idealism of the first President of the T.S.—Col. Olcott—and the mysterious and powerful personality of Madame Blavatsky, could not be disregarded. Apart from theories, there were also hints for developing the super-physical faculties latent in us. I began practising concentration and meditation according to the then newly published book by Ernest Wood. After some years of rather fruitless efforts my enthusiasm began to diminish. The exercises mentioned did not prove very effective. Among Theosophists I could not find men who really knew and could give me advice apart from printed books. Their Masters were not accessible, and seemed to be rather like a myth. It appeared that only Madame Blavatsky and Col. Olcott had had the privilege of meeting them in physical form. On my inquiry late in 1926, Mrs. Besant wrote to me: 'It is true that after the death of Col. Olcott in 1907, the Masters withdrew their direct guidance of the T.S., but recently in 1925, they resumed that guidance'.

At first the development of the superphysical faculties was interesting: it excited my curiosity. Afterwards I found that, being based on the changing physical being, they were subject to the currents of the mind and so were a blind alley—away from the supreme goal.

Then came studies in Hermeticism which is based on an ancient

49

Egyptian tradition, and uses the symbolism of the Tarot as one of its main features. Being mathematically minded, the relationship and connection between numbers and the Tarot cards engaged my attention. Eliphas Levi and Dr. Papus temporarily became my intellectual masters. I became engrossed in a cumbersome process of creating new thoughts and ideas by working with a pack of Tarot cards. I held meetings in public with the members of different occult societies. It delighted me to see the attentive faces of my listeners apparently following my conceptions and calculations with the help of drawings on the large blackboard behind my chair.

Then another step—the next meeting was devoted to the ancient Kabbalah. When I had finished, the blackboard was covered with Hebrew letters, mystical triangles and drawings. The lecture ended in loud applause.

In the audience I saw a friend—a retired general. He was then president of a metaphysical society and a most kind-hearted man. He said to me afterwards: 'Your lectures are very interesting and the hall is always full. The fact that the public obviously does not understand even ten per cent of the matter is apparently no hindrance to the success of the exposition'. These words gave me much food for thought, and as a result, I stopped public lecturing. I realized that ninety-nine per cent of the people came only to hear about something mysterious, from which they hoped to add some savour to their lives.

My activities with Hermetic occultism came to an end after performing a magical ritual as laid down by Eliphas Levi and Dr. Papus. Three of us prepared ourselves for twenty-one days. For the operation we chose a tower of an almost ruined castle in a remote area. The results were poor in proportion to the labour and time sacrificed. We succeeded, it is true, in obtaining some apparitions (spirits or elementals) in the smoke of incense and of special dried plants; also some audible phenomena and effects of perfume. But I was disappointed. The results could not possibly be tested scientifically and gave no ground for definite conclusions. Even the very impressions received, appeared different to each of us. Gradually I gave up the whole business of ceremonial magic.

My next study was of a very interesting book by Dr. Brandler Pracht, a German occultist. His method was definite and clear. He recommended many valuable exercises leading to the control of thoughts, and in consequence of the whole personality. Their aim was the acquiring of power and ability:

1. To concentrate the mind upon only one thing without deviation or gaps.
2. Deliberately to stop the whole process of thinking for ten minutes at a time.

There were, of course, many other instructions which cannot be described here. Strangely enough he expected one to reach the grade of a 'young master' in about six months. However, I spent much more time than that in order to obtain both kinds of concentration for only three minutes.

The period of Hermeticism, magic and Dr. Brandler Pracht, was behind me. I visited France. In Paris was the headquarters of the Association of Spiritual Friendships (Amitiés Spirituelles) of France, founded by Paul Sedir, for twenty years well known as an occultist and mystic. His most mysterious book—*The Initiations*—made a good impression on me. He wrote plainly about his Master, and later about his personal experiences with the so-called 'Master of Masters', the very name of whom he never dared to pronounce. This organization, being semi-secret, advocated the most elevated and pure ideas that I then knew. But at that time (1935) Paul Sedir had been dead for thirteen years. I therefore sought the Great Master described by him, but was unable to meet him. Eventually I found some old members who knew Sedir and who could possibly show me the path. It was a hard task, for the Western Masters purposely use a policy different from their Eastern Brothers. They prefer to be and remain completely unknown to all except their true disciples, and their inviolable standards are very high. It is extremely difficult to be allowed into the presence of these great beings, and the silence of secrecy must be sworn and observed for life. I cannot therefore say anything more.

There was one early experience which may be worth describing. Living in our town was a Bishop whom people described as a Saint. He was a true ascetic. People of all creeds came to him to ask his blessing, which was said to be very effective. I had to leave my university studies and enlist, for that was during the first world war, when I was nineteen. My mother was a keen Theosophist and had fine religious feelings. But as was natural at my age, I was concerned only with sport and study. One day my mother said to me: 'My son, you are going to the war. I do not know if the Almighty will grant me grace to see you again. Tomorrow I want to take you to our saintly Bishop. He will give you his holy blessing'.

Reluctant as I was, I could not refuse my mother's wish. So the next afternoon a priest took us into a modest room with only a few wooden chairs and a crucifix on the wall. The Bishop entered. I saw a thin man in his forties in the simple dress of a monk. His hands were joined on his breast and his head was somewhat bent. The strange wax-like complexion of the thin face was framed by long black hair falling to the shoulders. When he came closer I could see his eyes, dark, and filled with a strange, soft light. They were so different from those of any other human being, that I was struck by their mysterious expression of peace, power and wisdom. Fortunately I refrained from making any conventional greeting. It seemed as if I could not speak. But the Bishop smiled gently and said in a low voice: 'It is good young man, that you came here'. Then he raised his hands over my head and made a broad sign of the Cross. I spontaneously kissed his meagre hand. That was all. Leaving the room I could hear the words spoken to my mother, who was still before him: 'Go in peace. Everything will be well with the boy'.

And I remembered this moment again when I sat at the feet of Maharshi for the first time, soon after my arrival at the Ashram. Also I remembered as in a dream, that the christian name of the

Bishop was the same as that of the unknown master whom I had tried to meet in Paris years later.

Soon after my visit to France, family life, and later the Second World War, brought me to a period of darkness. I forgot all my previous endeavours. Not earlier than the spring of 1945 an elderly lady, with whom I sometimes spoke of Theosophy, lent me Paul Brunton's 'A Search in Secret India'. She literally forced me to take the book, for I was by no means eager to read it; but the last two chapters, where the author describes his visit to Maharshi, were decisive. At last I had found my true Master.

This certainty came of itself and permitted no doubts. And then I realized why all my previous searching had been in vain. The occult ways mentioned before were only blind alleys. They could give me some help, but there was no vision of the true goal. Therefore of necessity, they were unsuccessful. Their exercises, concentrations and breath controls absorbed only time and energy. They veiled the aim which I could not see in their shadows.

On the path given by the Great Rishi the goal is visible from the first step. It is spiritualization of the man. The power of the spirit is unlimited. Now it was clear to me why the Vichara (self-inquiry) could replace the time-devouring training of occult practices. All that I had previously been striving after—concentration, meditation, breath and body control, a clear vision of reality, peace and bliss—all of them now came of their own accord, as ripe fruit falls from a tree.

Then I began to work with Vichara as described later in Chapter XIV. The first steps are always the most difficult. Now I can laugh over these difficulties encountered when entering the Direct Path, but then it was almost an inner ordeal. And little wonder, for the whole inner world of a man must be changed and his mind subdued. The tragedy was that I knew that it must be done, but did not then know to 'whom' my former 'lord'—the mind—had to capitulate. There was an emptiness in me when I tried to exclude the thinking process from my consciousness. This emptiness was not pleasant and it even brought some fear. The feeling was similar to that of a mountaineer, who on entering higher regions feels that there is not enough air to breathe, and that he is suffocating. So I decided that I needed better conditions and more opportunity for meditation and Vichara.

I knew long before that if we think strongly for some days about a certain thing, at a certain time, we find that our thoughts return to it at the same hour and even minute. This helps to make our meditation easier and more effective and spares us much effort. I decided to use this means and at the same time to find more congenial conditions for study.

A friend in Paris, a Roman Catholic priest, a well-educated and elderly man with whom I sometimes corresponded, knew of my endeavours, without in any way attempting to dissuade me from them. I wrote to him saying that I wanted to find a place in which to live for some months, where quiet meditation would be possible. He kindly recommended his own monastery. Anyone, he said, who is a Roman Catholic and feels a need for spiritual concentration can go there for a time, take part in the simple life of its inmates and profit according to his own inner capacity. Intuitively I felt that this was what I was seeking.

In a few weeks I had arranged my affairs, was being ushered into the presence of the Prior and accepted as a temporary resident. There were no obligations on my side and I told him frankly that I contemplated leaving Europe in a few months for a country in the Southern Hemisphere. But I was told that Father N., my friend, had already given all particulars about myself and that everything was in order.

I was given a pleasant room in the vast building, which was a monastery in the heart of Paris. Another priest visited me and asked what books I would like to read. Very gently he suggested a study of the *Imitation of Christ* by Thomas a Kempis. He was immensely pleased when I told him that it was the very book for which I would have asked. Incidentally, he had it with him in the pocket of his cassock.

During the first weeks I was left completely alone. According to my plan I entered into the simple life of the monastery, and found it appropriate for my aims. In the morning before breakfast I went to the gallery on the first floor of the chapel. It ran around the interior of the church and there were chairs and many small altars where priests said masses every morning. Later I began to visit this quiet and peaceful place whenever I wished to meditate. After breakfast I studied in my room whatever I had as a special programme for the day. After lunch I sometimes went for a walk, visiting numerous famous places in the city.

In addition, I tried to train my mind, to rule it in the midst of the feverish life of this large city, and an explanation of the method used will be found in Chapter XIV.

Sometimes as dawn broke I would still be sitting on my chair in the half-dark gallery of the chapel, merged in meditation. One of the priests, a member of the monastery staff, seeing me sitting for long hours without movement, once visited me in my room and asked if such long and obviously intense meditations might not impair my health. Our body is a fragile instrument, said the good old man, and if we injure it, our capacity to serve the Lord is diminished. Of course I assured him that I knew what I was doing and how much my body could stand, but thanked him sincerely for his concern on my behalf.

I visited all the various departments of this great community, which is separated from the outside world by high walls. I spoke with cooks and servants, with gardeners and tailors. All were Brothers of the Order and everyone had his work. In the morning they assisted the priests at mass, and during the day interrupted their labours at fixed times for short prayers.

They were mostly simple men, devout and friendly, and had spent their lives since youth there. Sometimes they were transferred to other monasteries in the country. They accepted everything without question. Then I understood the meaning of 're-nunciation of one's own will' and its place in spiritual progress. It was but another form of extinguishing the old enemy, the so-called ego. This form and method is the best for simple and less educated people, from whose ranks come most of the Brothers of these Catholic religious orders.

When I asked them which they preferred—prayers or work for the community—they told me simply that their work was only another form of prayer.

Three years later, when in India, I was given a pamphlet written by a famous Indian Saint and Yogi, a highly educated man who has his own Ashram in the Himalayas. The title was: *'Work is worship. Dedicate it to God.'*

Now I could understand the unseen ties that bind all humans striving for the Highest. It dawned on me here, in one of the spiritual centres of the West, why I felt no disharmony, in following a path based on Eastern methods, in a temple consecrated to another great teacher, for whom I had always felt the deepest admiration and love.

About this time I came in contact with the head of the Ramakrishna Mission in Paris, the eminent Swami S., whom the Ashram of Sri Maharshi had recommended me to visit. He was always very busy, but when he was shown my letter from Tiruvannamalai, he immediately gave me an interview.

During our talk, he said: 'Sri Maharshi is your spiritual Master, your Guru. Ask him for help—it will be granted to you'. Also, pointing to the way out of some inner difficulties I had confessed to him, he gave me a short mantra which would put me in touch with the Great Rishi, whom of course, I had not yet seen. It was the repetition of 'Om, Ramana, Om'.

*　　　*　　　*

Months passed and my Vichara was firmly established, but it was not yet the living vital Vichara transforming the whole man, which it later became in South America. But even this had no comparison with the light which illumined it when I was in the presence of the Master Maharshi himself. And so I say that the great being who gave us this wonderful tool, in a form appropriate to our epoch—the Self-Inquiry or Vichara—becomes our beloved Master and Lord of our lives.

He has already merged in the infinite ocean of life, which is the universal reality, the spirit and pure being.

What else could be the ultimate destiny of us all, of you and me, who are really rivulets seeking the same ocean—our eternal home of bliss?

CHAPTER X

'As by Mixture with Water . . .'

'As by mixture with water and by friction, sandal-wood emits an excellent odour, removing all bad smells; so divine aspiration becomes manifest when external desire is washed away'.

From Sri Sankaracharya's *Viveka-Chudamani*

Today during meditation I remembered these words of Sri Sankaracharya, the greatest philosopher and spiritual teacher in India for the last 2,000 years.

The modifications in my consciousness are now so swift and imperceptible that the mind is unable to register them as they take place. I could note down only a few of the most important immediately after they occurred. One of them, probably the most significant, was this: although I cannot yet stay in contemplation the whole day long—this is obvious—yet I return to it without any effort as soon as I hear any of Maharshi's words, read something of his writings, or even those of any other Master who deals with the spiritual life. Till now it is chiefly casual, but I know that soon I shall be able to enter this state at will. Once the path is open, one cannot forget nor desert it. In the presence of the Saint the mind is tuned-up to silence, and does not dare to indulge in endless questioning as it used to do.

This blind egoistic element loses its power and charm in the presence of *one* who prevails over it and discovers its true *source*. Maharshi says clearly:

'The mind is constituted by thoughts. Stop thinking and show me then where is the mind?'

Experience proves, that after discarding all thoughts from what we call 'mind', *nothing* remains. But life does not stop there, as unfortunately, many people are apt to believe. On the contrary, it manifests itself with more power and intensity, although, it is true, far more subtly. I well remember those times when I could not imagine that one could exist without thinking. Maharshi says:

'The most important way to improve the mind is to stop thinking. Thinking and thinking is the cause of the heated brain'.

What is the practical difficulty in achieving this control? It lies in the fact that, for untrained people, the very process of thinking has in itself a charm not easy to overcome.

The constant inward use of Maharshi's question: '*Who am I?*' (called also 'Inquiry', in Sanscrit '*Vichara*') quiets the rebellious mind. One also sees that the acceptance of the axiom: 'No one has ever been able to discover truth by thinking, nor to arrive at any definite discovery in the spiritual realm through the activity of the mind', destroys the very interest in the process of thought itself. And when our interest weakens, we are not far from victory.

The more we become independent of our mind, compelling it to silence at will, the better the servant it becomes, and the more useful the services it can render to us in its own sphere of action. Many ignorant people, when they hear about the necessity of 'transcending the mind' or even 'killing it', imagine that such an action would result in a kind of dullness or stupor, rendering one incapable of solving the ordinary problems of life on the physical plane. But remember: 'The mind is a good servant, but a cruel master'.

It seems that 'to transcend the limits of the mind', which in practice, is tantamount to the transfer of consciousness to the transcendent spiritual level, is not possible for each and everyone. One may hear about the process and the methods of applying it, but may not necessarily understand, still less be inclined to follow the hints given. I have met many people, quite intelligent in the usual sense of the word, who were utterly incapable of imagining such a possibility, or of grasping, even in theory, the problem itself; just as we cannot perceive ultra-violet rays. All their life was concentrated on the physical plane, and on it alone could they see their purpose. The very conception of other possibilities, was for them non-existent. Of course these problems, as well as the present book, are not meant for this type of person.

*　　*　　*

An elderly Brahmin who is sitting near me is reciting the 'Gayatri', the most ancient Mantra of the Aryan race, for him a formula of daily meditation. I enter the current and mentally repeat with him:

Let us meditate upon the glory of the ONE who created this universe. Let him illumine our minds.

CHAPTER XI

Within the Ashram

It is a delicate task to write about people still living. Therefore this part of my diary will be limited to general observations. During my own stay at the Ashram, among Westerners represented, there were three Americans, two ladies and a gentleman; an Englishman who had been living in the compound for fourteen years; an English lady who came soon after my arrival; also some French people, a Jew, two Poles and a German. With few exceptions my time was fully occupied with my own problems and with Maharshi. I did not wish to enter any social life. The main meeting place was the hall of the Ashram, and naturally the temple where Maharshi spent most of his time giving Darshan.

Among the Indians the most interesting to me were the Swamis, the devotees by 'profession'. Some were intelligent and really devoted men. In the evening I would see some of them sitting at the nearby shrines, giving instruction to peasants from the town and surrounding villages. On the stone altars there were lights burning, and the Swamis sat on the steps, reciting holy scriptures and singing hymns.

There was a Muslim scientist, professor of an Indian University, with whom I had many chats. The postmaster of the Ashram was one with whom I also had many friendly talks. His childlike and kind attitude appealed to me, as did his limitless devotion to his great countryman, our beloved Bhagavan. I was afraid my correspondence was giving him much trouble, but he performed his duties as postman with ability and good will.

Scores of Brahmins and intelligentsia from all parts of India kept up a steady flow of visitors to Tiruvannamalai. Representatives of high Indian circles, Rajas and Maharajas with their families were also frequent guests. Some had European wives in beautiful and expensive saris. The Princes have a separate hostel

61

some hundred yards from the compound. They offer costly gifts to the Ashram and have contributed greatly to its construction.

There is no distinction made between the classes of Indian society in Maharshi's presence, but the staff provide places for Indian Princes near Maharshi, as they come only for one or two days.

The Ashram has a well-organized book-shop filled with its publications. But all these things are minor details and lack vital interest for me. The Master is the sun and all else revolves round him.

CHAPTER XII

Teachings of Maharshi

It is strange that we are compelled to recognize two apparently contradictory facts. The teachings of the Great Rishi of India are substantially as old as the first traces of philosophic thought and yet they open up a new world of spiritual achievement.

On the doors of the ancient initiation temples of Greece was an inscription 'Gnothi Seauton'—'Know Thyself'.

Plato repeated 'Know yourself and you will know the world and the Gods'. The Self-Inquiry of Maharshi—the mysterious Vichara—says the same. It is the keystone of his message for the modern world. We wonder wherein lies the power of that message, if the fact has been known for thousands of years. The solution is in the answer to another question:

Who gave us the teaching and *When*?

Maharshi is a contemporary Sage, and he is himself the living proof of the truth he brought from his own realm of spiritual experience. He discovered the Vichara when he knew nothing about religious philosophy. As a boy of sixteen, merged in the transcendental state of Samadhi, he reached realization of the Self—the ultimate truth—without aid. There was no doubt of truth for him, because he himself became that truth.

The writer and poet, Grant Duff (Douglas Ainslie) in his account of 'The Greatest Event in My Life' in the *Golden Jubilee Souvenir* (published by the Ramanasramam in Tiruvannamalai), tells of the striking effect felt when he first saw Sri Maharshi. He wrote: 'I saw Maharshi for the first time, but the moment he looked at me I felt he was the Truth and the Light'.

This experience was by no means exclusive to Mr. Grant Duff. Many others have felt it with an irresistible certainty of the soul. Therein lies the greatest mystery of the true realization of God—truth. For then a man becomes one with Him. And at the same time another miracle happens—that man is then closest to all other men.

It is difficult to express the sublime. I spoke with the Master only three times, and on each occasion only for a few minutes. No more was necessary. Speech was too clumsy and inadequate. In my last talk with him (see chapter 'Farewell') the reader will find that I intuitively kept silent.

When Gandhi sent Sri Rajendra Prasad, the present President of the Indian Republic to ask Sri Maharshi for a message, the latter said: 'Of what use are words when the heart speaks to the heart?' And the messenger went back to his Master, Mahatma Gandhi, satisfied with the answer of the Great Rishi.

So the Self-Inquiry—'Who Am I?'—was always the basis of all the teachings of Maharshi. He told us that while putting the inquiry to ourselves, we must clearly realize that our bodily senses and mind are impermanent and conditioned, and should be excluded from the realm of the real. Then that which remains unaffected by them will be the Self.

By the constant and firm use of the Vichara we come to the silence. During his long life on this earth Maharshi gave many commentaries on his teachings, in reply to questions put to him by innumerable visitors and disciples. They are written down in several books published by the Ashram. One of them, the incomparable *Maha Yoga* ('The Great Yoga'), contains all the essentials of his sayings classified in appropriate form by an eminent disciple. This book is indispensable to every earnest student of Maharshi's message. It is not my purpose here to quote from it. If you study it you will understand the message and the greatness of Maharshi.

A writer's usefulness and power to convince about spiritual matters depends on the mood and intuition with which he writes. We can express our mental conceptions, our problems and theories. They are the children of our outer mind, and they will be cold and stillborn unless breathed upon by the inner reality.

In an initiatory booklet by H. P. Blavatsky—*The Voice of the*

Silence—we read: *For mind is like a mirror; it gathers dust while it reflects'*.

And so, in a spiritual search, the role of the mind is a minor one. Writing with the outer mind only, we try to gather suitable words and choose ideas that are to go on paper. That is the mind's work. Then we remain for ever in the realm of the unreal, and the ultimate truth will be veiled indefinitely to us.

Maharshi taught us to use a different process: to refer to a higher level of consciousness, where all imperfections of the 'mirror' are transcended. That is the realm of the true Self, of the Over-Self. Writing from that level we do not choose our ideas or words. They come by intuition, already chosen as it were. An educated Brahmin reading these lines would smile and say: 'Dear Mouni, why do you not say what you mean, and call it simply the Buddhic consciousness?' But this will convey nothing to a reader not conversant with Indian classical terms.

The Sage of Arunachala also gave us another great injunction, that we should strive now to attain in this life that level of consciousness which transcends the 'normal'. For then we attain a consciousness which will endure for ever, independent of the death of the body. This state frees us from all fears and uncertainties. This is that 'pearl of great price', that 'treasure' worth any toil to discover, that 'good part' which shall not be taken from us.

Maharshi did not occupy himself with theories. A famous saying of his is: 'There is no reincarnation; there is no Ishwara (personal god); there is nothing; you have only to be'. This is the ultimate truth for those who attain the highest conception of unconditioned being. This plane can be attained because he attained it. I believe that the very purpose of a great being who comes for our sake to this earth is not so much to give us a 'new teaching' (if 'new teachings' ever exist), as to give an example of attainment, fulfilling the teachings of the sacred books and pouring new life into them.

Such is the purpose of the Maha-Yoga, confirmed over and over again by Maharshi himself.

E

The different religions of the world are designed for the average man. They gives rules of conduct for a good life, promising heaven afterwards as a reward. They are good in their own field The laws of cause and effect are true. They are natural laws. Generating good during our different forms of existence, we create propitious conditions for our further progress. But once we see the glorious goal of our existence, other petty aims lose their attraction, and we gradually become incapable of doing evil; for evil lies in the realm of our ephemeral and sense-conditioned ego, which Maharshi calls 'a hybrid arising between the true Self and the body'.

Another teaching on which he laid great stress is that there is no such thing as the evolution of spirit or of the Self. His conception is much more realistic and full of common sense. He says the real Self is ever present in us; only the shrouds of matter veil it. All that we have to do is to remove the illusion (Maya) and the Self will light up in us; there is no need to seek it elsewhere.

From what has been said above it may be taken for granted that the teachings of the Great Rishi will not be acceptable to everyone. Mankind up to a certain stage will always prefer living in the realm of matter and the senses. We cannot make a child instantaneously grow into an adult, nor can we pour a quart of water into a pint pot. In due course the child will grow. What is essential for those souls who are advanced enough is to take advantage of the presence of the Messenger. He gathers them around Him during His physical life, and helps them to take the last steps towards realization.

Before closing this chapter I would like to quote one more important statement of my Master:

'Your own Self-Realization is the greatest form of service you can render to the World'.

So do not worry if you cannot feed all the hungry and the poor. They have their own destiny, or as our Indian friends say, their own Karma. Be a blessing and a boon to everyone and everything that you encounter in this life, but do not go out of your Path to seek any special activity, for it may entangle you in this world of unreality, and you would then forget the goal.

Before you have attained realization it is always uncertain whether your activity is really sound. There is, however, one method of avoiding mistakes in your actions. It is, as the Master says, when you act without egotism—that is—when you do not believe any more that *you* do the work. This attitude is called by the author of *Maha Yoga* the Egoless state of consciousness.

'Have faith in God and in yourself; that will cure all. Hope for the best, expect the best, toil for the best and everything will come right for you in the end'.

From *Maharshi's Sayings.*

Grant me, Oh Lord, equality towards all, universal love and *association with the spiritual Master.*

CHAPTER XIII

The Direct Path

From what has already been said, it can be seen that the Great Rishi—unlike most yogis and many saints of the present day—does not recommend yogic practices *as a condition* for the highest and perennial spiritual achievement, called by him 'self-realization'. He dismisses from that aim, all the cumbersome postures, breathing exercises, control of the pranic currents (currents of the Prana in the human body and so of Nature itself), and so on. In fact, he seldom even mentions them in his talks.

So the Direct Path to spiritual attainment, as shown by the Maharshi, does not require any unnatural body postures, often so difficult to perform for the majority of people; none of the efforts of Hatha-Yoga, which can be dangerous unless practised under the direct supervision of a competent teacher, and no artificial mental practices of concentration. All such things lead nowhere unless accompanied by the elements of spiritual enlightenment, a fact which is firmly underlined by Sri Sankaracharya in his *'Viveka Chudamani'* ('The Crest Jewel of Wisdom').

Now I see clearly that these things belong to a closed and be-witched circle. For years I and some of my closest occult friends practised many kinds of 'outer-yogas' (I have coined this word to distinguish them from the Maha Yoga or Direct Path), but without any results worthy of our efforts. Of course, some of these exercises were good for our physical health, especially for stilling the nerves, cultivating a beautiful voice, and so forth. But these advantages only remained with us as long as we continued regularly to perform the exercises. A pause for even a few weeks deprived us of all the hard-earned benefits we had gained at the cost of such effort and waste of time. No true and permanent peace of mind could be obtained, although for that purpose I made intense use of Japa (repetition) with the best of mantras. Just as

68

Paul Sedir, the eminent French occultist and writer who was later converted to spirituality, asked in his *Initiations*: 'And what of eternal values did I learn from all the years I spent on the study of the so-called "Secret Science"?'

The Master Sri Maharshi says the same and much more. He states that the control of the mind, achieved by *any way except the Vichara* (Self-Inquiry) will be *only temporary*, for the mind *will invariably return to its spontaneous activities*. 'What is not natural', says the Sage, 'cannot be permanent, and what is not permanent is not worth striving after'. What reasonable person would disagree with the Great Rishi? Who cannot see that there is no possibility or hope of realization if undertaken with inadequate methods? For then one simply has no time for the proper work with the only instrument, the Vichara. Life is too short to waste when we are working earnestly towards achievement. Moreover, for the majority of aspirants in both East and West, complicated occult practices invariably require quite a different and usually too difficult rearrangement of everyday life. These hundreds of exercises, postures, prayers, invocations and meditations, are all incompatible with the resources and possibilities of an average person's normal life. Few aspirants possess sufficient wealth to allow them to retire completely from the outer activity of this visible world and lead the necessary passive existence. No working or family-man or woman could lead such a life without becoming a social burden to others, which is inadmissible for one who strives high. In the majority of Western countries, it would be unthinkable to lead a beggar's life—as is possible in the East—without coming into conflict with the Law, and that would be wrong.

But this Direct Path, the Maharshi's way, is possible and is well suited for everyone who is ripe enough to enter on it, no matter whether man or woman, young or old, rich or poor, learned or illiterate. This Path can be followed secretly, so that the outer world will never know that a man is engaged in a deep and intensive search. This means that there is a reduction to the minimum of external obstacles allowed by the prarabdha karma of man.

Also there is no question of reading innumerable books, which are usually written by men who themselves could never hope to practise all that they try to suggest to their followers. For there is *one thing* by which, when It is cognized, everything becomes clear and known; but without It, all else remains in the realm of ignorance, and reality, unchangeable existence or life, cannot be reached.

That is why so small a number of aspirants are able to achieve anything worth the mention, apart from the rather useless filling of the mind with thoughts and theories borrowed from others. Merely watching others eating will not satisfy our own hunger. We must eat for ourselves if we wish to live.

The multiplicity of theories with their countless books, the many sects and religions with their almost invariable hostility to one another—no matter how cleverly this unpleasant quality is disguised—all show a lack of unity which is only a proof that there is little or no truth in any of them.

But the Direct Path immediately gives us a clear view of our ultimate and only aim. The process of acquiring virtues is reversed. We do not need to seek them, for they come according to the measure of our advancement along the path. I cannot help but remember Christ's words about the kingdom of heaven, which *must* be sought *before* all else: 'Seek ye first the kingdom of God and his righteousness; and all these things shall be added unto you'. To compel ourselves to seek virtues is practically as useless as to fly from temptation. We all know that no true victory can be won by flight, but only by vigorous and courageous fighting. And we should know what we are fighting against, otherwise we will lose. It is only the Direct Path which tells us from the first step, *where* we are going and *why*. Our *renunciation* of this unreal world, while *not usually known* to those around us, acquires a *natural* and reasonable character, and not that of imagination or of a hazy dream. Then we know experientially the true value of the things among which we still live.

When meditating about all this, I see that many of the popular contemporary writers on Yoga and occultism are not 'masters' of the realm they try to describe. While promising their followers all sorts of control over their bodies and lives, they themselves have not achieved such control. Allegedly they know all about Yoga and the hidden powers in man, but often a glance is sufficient to see how far they are from the claimed 'control' and even from bodily 'perfection', much less of higher things. It is so much easier to write books than to achieve realization of the truth. 'Physician first cure thyself!'

I realize that many people must still follow these doubtful ways, for they are unable to appreciate the unique one, which leads to the ultimate achievement. And in that sense we can accept—to a certain degree—that 'All paths lead to the same goal', for time itself is flowing away through eternity.

If we have a fast car at our disposal, it is highly improbable that we will prefer to use the sort of bullock-cart which I see in Tiruvannamalai every day. And yet this type of ancient conveyance has been in use here for thousands of years and still serves the present-day villagers quite well. So there is nothing wrong with them from the point of view of time.

Now things are different. If I no longer need any books, it is because the very source of initiation is here before my eyes. This is a position enjoyed by but a few men, and I know it will last for only a short time. But where is that power, which could destroy the glorious realization of the presence of a true Master?

The beautiful words of another great teacher intuitively enter my consciousness: '*I am the way, the truth and the life: no man cometh unto the Father, but by me*'. In the presence of Maharshi this mystical truth becomes clear and real. For here, at the feet of Bhagavan, I see, as have others before me, that *He is the path*.

The Direct Path is also a fulfilment of the spiritual testament of the Lord Buddha: 'You cannot destroy your illusion by creating another in its place'. The Master of the Direct Path now sitting on his couch before me, is the greatest destroyer of all illusions.

Under no circumstances can one who saw his light, continue to believe in the illusion of this unreal but manifested universe, which as the Master says, exists only in our mind. Then the poison of the compromise between the theoretical acceptance of the above truth and the actual practice of it in everyday life, is for ever excluded.

Another quotation comes to mind; it is from *The Voice of the Silence* by H. P. Blavatsky, which is based on the foremost mystic work of Northern Buddhism: 'The Self of Matter and the Self of Spirit can never meet. One of the twain must disappear; there is no place for both'. The Direct Path agrees with this.

Sri Maharshi apparently supports the Advaita-Vedanta theory which recognizes only one real thing, the Atman, self or spirit. In his *Viveka Chudamani*, Sankaracharya says: 'All this universe, known through mind and speech, is the spirit . . .' If we follow the development of this philosophy to its root, we will see that the evanescent material counterpart of man is as if non-existent. Also, we can recognize that Advaita is in advance of the above quoted verse from the *Voice of the Silence*, because the material self (or triple ego as we know it) is considered as utterly unreal and without existence.

Now from my former multiplicity of conceptions, I come to the *one*, which is a substitute for all of them and which answers or perhaps *annihilates* all my questions. And this is how the coveted peace of mind is achieved. In practice, how different is the Path leading to it in contrast to my former struggling.

When we realize that there exists an infallible path to the final goal, the joy of that knowledge is overwhelming. This is the water which quenches human thirst; for humanity is never left without some remedy or assistance in its trials and wanderings. Those who seek—find. But the search must be for the highest and not merely for more or less exalted illusions. The cardinal virtue of discrimination plays an uppermost role in such seeking. For when the Direct Path becomes visible, all the others disappear as if they had never been sought. There is no need for any 'rejection' on the part of the disciple. He simply seems to forget what is best forgotten and remembers only what should be remembered.

Deep in our hearts there lies a source, so often spoke of by the

Master. It can be likened to the centre of a circle, from which we can see in all directions, and then from which no other position can give us such a vantage point. Now I fully realize why the path of Maharshi is also called the Path of Inner Silence. To whom would speak the *only seer*?

Go directly to the source of all truth in your spiritual centre of silence, your heart; for the shortest distance between two points is a direct line, and a mystical truth lies hidden behind this geometrical axiom. Accept it, and the Direct Path is already beneath your feet. There is no need to seek It elsewhere. 'A single step begins the journey of a thousand miles', but if this 'first step' is not taken, the traveller will remain at his starting point.

Without the knowledge of 'who we are', we remain spiritually immovable. Sooner or later we must come to the true beginning and lose all memory of our previous wanderings.

The Direct Path can be likened to a mighty river, quietly and majestically flowing to the infinite ocean of Nirvana, Brahman, the Kingdom of Heaven, no matter what we call the ultimate and unique aim of every being. Yogas, religions, sects, philosophical systems, occult and spiritual societies, all can be thought of as minor streams flowing into and yielding up their waters to the same great river, and from then onwards having the same straight course to the ocean. But until they reach the direct current and are no longer separate, these streams of themselves cannot take anyone using them to the goal. Before they reach the main river, waterfalls, sandbars, and other irregularities may change the lie of their beds. And so, when swimming in or sailing on them, we cannot see the unique stream, which still lies hidden round their bends. Every moment brings yet another glimpse of the shore and other distant turnings. We tend to forget that everything has an end and so it will be with our by-paths. But whoever knows of the hidden Direct Path will not waste time following lesser ways. All efforts will be concentrated on the one idea 'How to enter the great current which flows directly to the ocean?'

It is possible that such people have already passed the twisted by-paths in former lives, and their experience now leads them to the ultimate highway, so that side-streams hold no attraction for them. From time to time, a Master steers His vessel on the great river and he sees those who have finished travelling along the smaller streams and are awaiting the last journey. From them he selects those who are fit and His ship disappears on the waves of Eternity.

The invisible ship is still sailing for us to 'see'. Its Master is willing to take us with Him.

CHAPTER XIV

The Technique of Vichara

The simplest things are sometimes the most difficult to achieve.

When we try to shut out all the whims and fancies of our restless mind, and to concentrate on the one chosen for a definite purpose, the mind fights desperately in order to resist control. It depends upon our will, who wins this fight. *Find out who is the creator of thoughts—and you have achieved the goal.* Such is true realization. But it is too mystical and needs relentless effort for its understanding. I began to work with Vichara for years before I met Maharshi, and the method according to his teachings is as follows:

To immerse oneself in meditation, making a clear impression on the outer mind that the real Self cannot be any transient thing such as the body, emotions or mind. When this fact is strongly established without any doubt in consciousness, then I try to fill every possible moment with the inquiry 'Who Am I?' When any other thought enters the mind one crushes it with the Vichara. The more determined the perseverance, the better the result. The restless mind begins to give up the struggle. As I substitute every approaching thought with the magic Vichara, the periods of absolute quietness become longer. At first it is only for a few seconds, but with constant practice there come minutes of unruffled peace. The most important thing is to catch and remember what was most helpful in reaching that peace of mind. I cannot describe that process in my consciousness, because it is above and beyond the activity of the mind, and therefore cannot be expressed in words, which belong to the mental realm. But each earnest student will have the same experience.

Wherever I was, Vichara was with me: walking in the street, sitting in trams and trains, in fact all day long when my mind was not immediately engaged in some necessary activity.

During the first months I counted the inquiries putting a number after each one. 'Who Am I?' (one), 'Who Am I?' (two), and so on. When circumstances compelled me to break the work, I noted the number in my memory, or if the break had to be longer, I wrote it on a slip of paper carried in my pocket for the purpose. For the first few days the figure of 1,000 was the highest. Later 7,000 and more became an easy mark. When I learned to fill every moment with Vichara excepting those of speech and compulsory mental occupation, the counting was discarded as unnecessary, for then the mind had learned to remember Vichara automatically. The important part was not to repeat Vichara with the mind, but to saturate each inquiry with a strong desire (without words) to know 'Who Am I?'.

Then the results were: peace of mind, and a power to use it after my own will, as a force apart from the individual 'I'. The average man believes, in his ignorance, that his body, emotions and mind constitute himself. The disciple trained by a Master overcomes this falsehood. And this is the turning point in his spiritual development, being a *sine qua non* for his progress on the path. Being under dominance of his mind the man is only a slave, and realization is not possible for those enslaved by the mind or the senses.

The spiritual aspect of Vichara is also clear. In using it you are seeking your *legitimate inheritance*, aiming directly at the very source of life. Other experiences made possible by the use of the inquiry 'Who Am I?' are given in other chapters. The whole problem of life is wrapped up in the Vichara. Every religion and every spiritual Master affirms that life in its essence is eternal and indestructible; but *what is that life?*

Maharshi reveals, and the disciple realizes, that eternal life is none other than *uninterrupted consciousness*.

To reach that state means to reach the immortality of spirit, of reality. That is the goal and the ultimate aim. There is nothing else. Meditate upon this and the truth will be made clear even to the outer mind.

Such are the heavens promised to the righteous and the saint, as told to us by Christ. For them there is no death any more. How clear now are the words of the great teacher of humanity !

And from the other aspect, it is clear why, for an undeveloped human being, there are and must be periodical interruptions in consciousness, connected with suffering and the fear of death.

If the highest level of consciousness in man does not transcend that of mind (and so it is for the majority of men), then this very factor implies incarnation in matter (Maya) and death, seen as transition into different forms with unavoidable temporary darkness and gaps in consciousness. But when our consciousness reaches the supra-mental realm, the realm of the eternal unchangeable spirit-self, the unchanging reality, then death is simply transcended and does not exist any more. Now can be understood the truth of the sayings of the Great Rishi, when he denies reincarnation in the realm of spirit, but otherwise speaks about it as an established fact. From his point of view both death and reincarnation are only illusions, and do not affect the real Self, just as our body is not affected by a change of dress. The Vichara throws light on every path.

CHAPTER XV

'Martha, Martha, thou art careful . . .

. . . Martha, Martha, thou art careful and troubled about many things: But one thing is needful: and Mary hath chosen that good part, which shall not be taken away from her'.

The invisible, but in its influence the most efficacious, light emanated by Maharshi brings about a total change in our opinions and in our appreciation of all the values of worldly life. After the few weeks I have spent here, I see so clearly the tragic emptiness of the slogans used by most people only to conceal the inner void and utter futility of their existence. I remembered having asked many people what they regarded as the chief purpose of their lives. Almost all the answers seemed to follow a certain common pattern, as if they had been turned out of a standard mould. Their gist was more or less as follows: 'The chief purpose of my life is to serve my nation; to help the progress of humanity; to assist the evolution and cultural development of my progeny; to give a good education to and inculcate moral principles in my children', and similar meaningless, insincere truisms. I preferred the simpler and more frank answer: 'My aim is pleasure. I want to enjoy life to the full while there is still time'.

I now understand that a being who does not know 'who he is' cannot have any right judgment, nor any idea about the things which transcend his personality. Also, that until human beings reach self-awareness, each one of them, without exception, is carried along by an automatic movement which he calls 'life', aiming at more or less short-termed goals.

The politician working, as he believes, for the prosperity of his state or nation, never ponders over the question as to whether the existence of this particular state or nation is necessary for the welfare of the universe as a whole, or whether it will not disappear after some time to give place to other entities of a similar kind. He even fails to realize, that the whole of our planet is not eternal, that everything on it, created through the ages by the countless generations of 'thinking beings' (as we like to call our brethren in evolution) will turn into dust, without leaving the slightest trace of itself behind, just as no life now remains on that 'dead' globe, the moon.

Actually, this understanding does not appear in such a definite form, or in such ready-made sentences as those I have written above. But I cannot find any other suitable way to express that realization which, in its pure essence, comes perhaps from the intuition, and is far beyond all words. Hence any attempt to try to express the meaning of this understanding born from the 'spiritual silence', must inevitably fail.

All the varieties of human activity down here have their source in the personality or ego. We know that both actor and action are equally illusory, and have no real existence save in the three-score years of ephemeral life spent in this physical body. If we grasp this fact we see all the unreality of our actions and achievements on the physical plane, which are at the basis of our personalities. The man who relinquishes his personality for the sake of the real ceases to be a slave of his illusions, and no longer believes in their usefulness, just as he cannot admit that his shadow can exist independently of his physical body.

'Vanitas Vanitatum et Omnia Vanitas'
Vanity of Vanities and all is Vanity'

This was quoted from Ecclesiastes by one of the inspired anchorites of Christianity, and the author of that marvellous book *The Imitation of Christ*. It is one more proof that 'All roads lead to Rome', in other words, in the spiritual realm all efforts to find truth, irrespective of creed, lead to the same final achievement.

When, about five years ago, I first discovered the teachings of Maharshi, I was struck by their resemblance to those of Thomas a Kempis, for many years well known to me. Now, in the presence of Light in a visible form, one understands even more clearly the basic unity of all the spiritual teachers of humanity. It is the ordinary men who have buried, in the grave of dogmas and transient commandments, the living, spiritual truth of Their teachings.

Belief in the 'superiority' of any religion does not exist for one who sits at the feet of a true Master of Wisdom. Maharshi also speaks about the 'ultimate truth', but this transcends all creeds and can be reached only by the few.

CHAPTER XVI

The Last Photographs of the Master

During the last few days, several leading photographers have come to take Maharshi's photograph. He obeys the requests of the 'specialists'—made in a most delicate and reverential way——and takes the various postures they ask him to assume, always with his kind, friendly and indulgent smile.

Of course, I thought, everyone knows that these are the last months of Maharshi's stay with us. Hence, they want to have the picture of the physical form of the Saint before it is too late. And the photographs are marvellous indeed. His face during these last years of his earthly life has the exquisite expression of an almost divine loving kindness, which stands out even more dominantly than the wisdom and power which are so prominent in his former pictures.

Some good photographs of the Master are available. Perhaps the best known was taken some sixteen years ago: it shows his face against the background of a kind of luminous cross, formed by the reflection of light. Another one well known to all readers of books on Maharshi, shows him in a classical Yogic posture, sitting cross-legged on a platform covered with a tiger skin. It was probably taken after his monthly shaving, for the features are free of the white beard, and both the purity of line and expression of incomparable power are emphasized more than in any other picture. Contemplating it we see a certain gravity on the face of the Saint who has for so long left behind him all the weaknesses, imperfections and miseries that reign among us. It shows one who has forever transcended all ignorance, and now faces the highest reality where no doubts or fears can exist. Every month after the shaving takes place I have the inestimable privilege of contemplating the features of the living form itself with its clear-cut lines—this marvellous head that is surrounded by a subtle

F

fragrance of incense and the still more subtle aroma of the utter devotion and love of hundreds of hearts.

One also perceives in this face that quality which is so rare in our brother men—infinite understanding. It is difficult to explain, but when one is in the presence of the Saint, one has the certainty that the whole of our being lies open and bare before him, and that he sees into its very depths. Of course, all this might not be quite pleasant or comfortable for the majority of people were it to happen before eyes other than those of the Maharshi. But in his presence no secrets can exist, nor does one have the slightest fear of criticism.

He is like the highest tribunal of our conscience, the Father-Confessor whose 'very presence purifies us from all sin', as was said about forty years ago by his friend, a Hindu Saint and clair-voyant, Seshadri Swami.

The third well-known photograph represents the face of the Master in a halo of white hair and beard, with a soft smile of ineffable tenderness.

Maharshi's mission on this earth is nearing its end. The oral teachings have been transmitted, transcribed and published by disciples and faithful friends. A group of 'initiates' remains to spread the words of wisdom further for those who are able to hear and accept them. Now remains only the cross of final martyr-dom, whose extent and purpose are unknown and inexplicable to us.

It was not my privilege to see its stages on the physical plane. I was told that the magnitude of Maharshi's physical suffering was terrible for those surrounding him. I believe that the all-wise Providence knows best as to what are the limits of our strength and endurance in any period of life.

This third picture of the Sage, which I contemplated every day during the whole of my stay in the Ashram, remained with me, for ever engraved on my heart, not only in its outward appear-ance, but infinitely more.

Just before the end, in April, 1950, the Master said to those around him: '*They say I am dying, but I shall remain here more alive than ever*'. Verily the Spirit of Maharshi has remained with us.

The photographs of Maharshi are now known all over the world. But how many people know the light which was brought by him from the realm of absolute bliss, the land of the highest spirit, and of the thorny paths, which are so narrow and difficult for most of us? Why are we so blind? Why are we unable to see this peace and bliss, wisdom and love, expressed so clearly even in the physical features of one who abides in that land forever? How much more resplendent must be that light there, where it is not veiled by the vehicles of matter, where shines the never-setting *sun*, about whose luminous rays every being dreams in the innermost depths of his heart.

CHAPTER XVII

One Operation More

For a few days rumours had been going round the Ashram that another operation is soon to take place to cut out the malignant tumour, whose growth has become so terrifying, weakening the whole body of the Sage. Last night several surgeons came from Madras with bags full of instruments. They assisted at the evening meditation and exchanged a few words with the Saint before leaving the temple hall.

This morning Maharshi was absent from his usual place, and the members of the Ashram staff said that the operation has to take place about noon.

All Westerners were on the alert, and many people were wandering round the temple, going here and there in the vicinity of the dispensary where the operation was being performed.

In the evening we were told that the operation was over, but Maharshi was very weak and would not be able to leave the dispensary. Later he sat in an arm-chair on the verandah of its white building, surrounded by surgeons and the Ashram staff, and on the nearby square a long queue had been formed by those who were anxious to see the Master. One by one they advanced, silently mounted the few steps, saluted, and immediately went down by the other side.

I was not there. I went to the temple, sat in my usual place and plunged into meditation, with no thoughts, no mental forms, in the quietness of that *silence* which is more eloquent than words. How marvellous is the peace of such a silence! It is beyond all the limits of time and human memory. It cannot be immediately interpreted in words, because of a certain reluctance on our part to touch this silence by thought. It does not allow us to use words until later.

These pages, therefore, were written after some time had elapsed, generally during the 'free' hours following lunch, when everyone goes to rest, all the life of the Ashram seems to be suspended and no one is in the temple hall. People generally sleep from noon to 3 p.m. But not myself, for I have much correspondence: letters reach me from all parts of the world in many languages from people of different nature, temperament and level of mental development.

Heat discourages all physical movement, but the super-physical functions remain independent of it, and the mind works normally. When I finish my correspondence for the day, I take my diary, or a few pages of my *Remembrances from India*, which I am trying to write in a form suitable for the average layman. I do not quite like it and have taken it up without enthusiasm. Some will see in it an almost trivial type of description, others will think it exaggerated and biased. All this cannot be helped.

A few days after the operation Maharshi appears in the temple hall; at first for a few hours only, then for a somewhat longer period, until finally, the usual routine is restored for a time.

Pupils and devotees as well as admirers come from all parts, probably to say farewell to the Master and have his final Darshan. Among them are Indians, and Westerners of many nations. They are chiefly elderly people, coming for a short stay of perhaps a few days. Among them there are serious as well as somewhat grotesque figures. One of the old disciples of Maharshi, the famous Yogi Ramiah, has remained almost two months in the Ashram. Every morning and evening he sat literally at the feet of the Master. Silent and dispassionate, wrapped in his white garments, he stayed quiet and motionless.

After the operation Maharshi is still thin, but a slight improvement is visible. Among the surrounding people optimistic rumours are spreading. Some expect a miracle, while others hope for better results from new methods of treatment.

I do not try to brood over the future. I am concentrated on the present, leaving the possible sorrow in store for the time when the Master will not be with me any more—of course, in the physical sense. But I know that I am seeing him in his physical body for the last time.

CHAPTER XVIII

Visiting Caves

I use part of the time when Maharshi is absent from the temple hall
to visit holy places in the vicinity. My first is to the sacred hill,
Arunachala, which rises high above the Ashram, as if pointing to
heaven with its sharp peak. I go to all the caves where the Sage
dwelt in his youth. One of the most famous is called 'Virupaksha'
cave. Here the young Swami Ramana spent many years in meditation and ascetic discipline. It is said that in ancient times a great
Yogi was buried there.

I easily found a little path on the slope of Arunachala leading to
this cave. There I saw a big rock jutting out and below it a small
verandah with a concrete floor, an iron lattice all round, and small
doors in the background. These were shut by a rusted and old, but
still used, lock. There were no signs of life. I went round the cave,
plucked a few red flowers and then sat quietly on a big warm
stone. As I was deciding to return home, a thin, middle-aged
Hindu came down from the hill and approached the cave. He
saluted me in the usual Hindu manner, to which I responded by
the same salute, placing my palms together at the level of my chest.
He opened the little iron gate and entered, inviting me with a kind
gesture and smile to follow him. I had to bend almost double to
pass through the very low and narrow doors.

Inside, in the centre of the little nine-by-nine-foot cell hollowed
out of the rock, stood a small cubic altar about five feet high
covered with garlands of wild yellow flowers. In the centre, blue
blossoms were scattered and a light was burning. On a shelf cut
out of the rock stood an earthen water-pot. By it my new friend,
the Sannyasin, placed the small vessel containing food which he
had just brought. Nothing else was to be seen in the cave. I sat
down on the cleanly swept concrete floor near the stone altar. My
host did the same. We understood each other without the need of

words. He knew the purpose of my visit and I understood well what this secluded, silent hermitage meant for him.

In the afternoon I went to another cave, situated somewhat higher up the hill, and named 'Skandashram'. This was the next place where Maharshi stayed before he came down to the present Ashram, where the grave of his mother, the temple and all the buildings are now situated.

As in Virupaksha the rock platform is surrounded by a lattice wall, and from a palm grove and small garden a few steps cut into the rock lead to a large verandah and several rooms inside. It was a Hindu holy day, and several festively dressed women and boys were standing on the verandah under the pleasant shade of the palms. A young Indian, with an intelligent and kind expression, came out to meet me. He showed me a small door leading inside. This cave was similar to, but looked a bit 'richer' than, the former one. An identical little altar stood in the centre adorned with flowers. A light was burning, and an old photograph of Maharshi, in a meditation posture and probably taken some forty years ago, was standing on the altar. Some mats with coloured stripes were stretched on the floor.

The young ascetic stood with folded hands and bowed head before Maharshi's picture. I inquired whether this was the room where the Sage had dwelt many years ago, as there were other little cells in the rock hermitage. He nodded assent, then went out for a moment, returning with a tray full of fresh ashes and a tiny vessel with the red powder called 'kum-kum'. Both are always used during Puja (Hindu ritual worship). One had to make a small mark between the eyebrows with the red powder, and then three stripes on the forehead with the holy ashes. The first was easy, but at the second I hesitated, not being sure how many stripes I must make, nor how to do so without risk of a mistake. The Swami who was holding the tray understood my uncertainty and immediately demonstrated with a kind gesture—three stripes were to be done with three fingers. I followed his example and after having complied with this ancient Aryan ritual sat down quietly in the corner of the verandah, near the Maharshi's former cell, and with-drew my consciousness from all objects, removing everything from its field. First the coloured saris of the women sitting opposite disappeared, then the whisper of an old white-bearded ascetic repeating his Mantras just near me.

When I 'returned' to the visible world I heard from afar the Ashram gong calling for supper. Here in the evening air, sounds are clearly heard for a radius of several miles. I silently took leave of the inmates of Skandashram and walked down the stony steps. So this evening, for the first time, I sat at the Ashram meal with the signs on me of a Hindu Sadhu, indicating a person dedicated to spiritual life. Maharshi's place was empty.

But opposite me sat the newly-arrived family of a Maharaja, his wife and two youngsters, his son and daughter. On the left was Yogi Ramiah's place, and on the right the senior pupils and the inmates of the Ashram. It seemed to me that the Maharaja's family were casting somewhat envious glances at my spoon which was so comfortable to use, especially when dealing with liquids, for out of courtesy, they had to follow the common custom of eating with the hand, whereas when at home they had probably long ago forsaken it.

CHAPTER XIX

Arunachala by Day

Arunachala means 'The Hill of Light'. According to an immemorial custom, on the day of Siva's festival called 'Kartikai' a big
fire fed with ghee (melted butter) is lit on the very top of Arunachala by the priests of the great Tiruvannamalai temple about a
mile from the Ashram. The light is seen for miles all round, as the
hills stands solitary on the plains. The festival is celebrated every
year in November. The legend says that many thousands of years
ago, Siva Himself appeared on the hill-top as a column of fire, and
since that time the Kartikai festival has always been celebrated.

That is the physical, the visible side of it, but the esoteric significance is far richer and deeper. Maharshi called Arunachala: the
reflection of the divine absolute bestowing liberation on those who
strive sincerely for it. He also said it represents our true Self, the
essential reality, the spirit, and the ultimate goal of our existence,
or the Atman. The Sage said clearly that though from the material
point of view, Arunachala is only a senseless hill, 'a mass of rocks
and stones'—understood in its real aspect, it is a symbol of the
highest being. I cannot here detail all the mythology connected
with the holy hill. I shall merely quote in a free translation, some
significant words of the Master:

'I discovered that the very thought about Arunachala, its mental
picture, stops the movements of the thinking principle and gives
the peace of achievement to the one who turns towards it.

There exists in the world a marvellous potion, for those who
have understood the ephemeral nature of worldly things and want
to discard this form of life. This rare potion does not kill the
physical man, but destroys his false, separate personality, if he can
only turn his thoughts towards it. Know that it is none other than
this Holy Hill—Arunachala. One who constantly asks himself:
Who Am I, what is the Source of me? One who plunges into the

depths of his being and finds the roots of the mind in the Heart, he himself becomes a Lord of the Universe, O Arunachala, Ocean of Bliss . . .'

I want also to give the literal version:

'I have discovered a New Thing! This Hill, the lodestone of lives, arrests the movements of any one who so much as thinks of it, draws him face to face with It, and fixes him motionless like Itself to feed upon his soul thus ripened. What a wonder is This! O Souls beware of It, and live! Such a destroyer of lives is this magnificent Arunachala, which shines within the Heart!

How many are there, who have been ruined like me for thinking this Hill to be the Supreme? Oh, Men! Disgusted with this life of intense misery, ye seek a means of giving up the body. There is on earth a rare drug which without actually killing him, will annihilate anyone who so much as thinks of it. *Know that it is none other than this Arunachala*'.

(From a Hymn by Maharshi translated by a member of the Ashram.)

These mystical words of the Sage have a deep meaning and also give some practical hints, but only for those who are consciously aiming at Liberation. For these the veil of words is lifted and only then can they see the mystic *light* of Arunachala shining forth in their hearts.

I begin to understand the meaning of the words: 'All the movements of the mind are stopped by Arunachala'. It is difficult to convey, save to him who has experienced it, but it is a fact that even the picture of the strange shape of the Hill of Light, seen by our mind's eye, or the very remembrance of Arunachala when one is far from it, helps in a concentration which is not only the beginning but a very condition of our advancement towards the Goal.

Today, taking advantage of Maharshi's absence from the hall, I have decided to explore the physical aspect of the hill. It means a climb to its summit. The weather is propitious as the sky is cloudy and there is not the usual heat. A strong and rather fresh wind also helps my enterprise, which is not at all easy, for I do not know the way and the slopes are steep and wild. It is difficult to see the path. In addition the appearance of things from a distance is different from what it is when one actually reaches them. Places which, from the plain, seem quite easy to climb, prove on approach impossible to scale. This was the greatest difficulty of my adventure.

Looking at the hill from below and following more or less a straight line, I traced my way through the slopes above the town of Tiruvannamalai and the Ashram. On the whole I climbed almost all the time, and generally at an angle of 45 degrees. I had to jump from one stone to another, avoiding the high dense weeds which grew profusely between the rocks, as within them might be hidden snakes or scorpions, so common in these parts.

Soon the town, the great temple with its towers, and the buildings of the Ashram became toys and the goatherds who were looking up at me from the lower slopes seemed like ants.

I noticed that the descent might be more difficult, for the stones, polished by rain and wind during the centuries, are round in shape and loosely embedded in the ground. Often they become dislodged and roll down the sides of the hill.

After half an hour's climb I reached a rock, which, seen from below, appeared to be about half way; but now looking up to the peak, I saw that the distance yet to climb was more than double that which had been left behind. Moreover the rock was so steep that there was no possibility of clambering over it with the aid only of the light bamboo stick I was carrying. It was lying directly across my chosen track, barring the way, and it seemed impossible to go round it.

I saw that the seemingly easy valleys leading to the rocky peak were neither near nor easy to climb. At last I understood that I was not on the proper path, and remembered the words of the chemist in Tiruvannamalai, who said that the best way is opposite Siva's temple, somewhat to the North. But it was too late now to find it. The only thing left, if I wanted to proceed and not to abandon my day's adventure, was to follow an almost invisible little track through the bushes and herbs on the left of the rock. It might prove to be longer, but there was no choice. I ceased looking where to step, as I had been doing before, because it took too much time. I thought: if a cobra has to bite me, no care of mine can possibly prevent it. I simply fixed my attention on Arunachala and after one hour reached the summit.

Sitting on a stone near the place where the famous Fire is lit—it was easy to recognize it by the black fatty patch made by the burned ghee—I remenbered Maharshi's advice as to how we should look at the material side of life, not allowing it to interfere with our constant search for light.

'Raise your head high. Do not look down on the tossing stormy sea of transient life. Else it will engulf you in its muddy waves. Fix your gaze aloft until you see the Splendid Reality'.

The literal translation is:

'Aim high, aim at the highest, and all lower aims are thereby achieved. It is looking below on the stormy sea of differences that makes you sink. Look up, beyond these and see the One Glorious Real—and you are saved'.

From Maharshi's Sayings

I meditated upon the fact that humanity is seeking happiness and light, new teachings and new teachers. And yet so many marvellous truths are at its disposal in all the religions of the world, and in the sayings of the mystics and masters, that even one lifetime would not be enough to know them all. And in reality one single maxim, if put into practice, suffices to guide us to the right path.

CHAPTER XX

'The I-Current'

Apart from Maharshi himself, this is a most mystical phenomenon. It is difficult to describe it in non-technical language. If we accept the fact that in Nature there is no loss of energy, then we can realize that spiritual forces generated by the meditations and radiations of the Samadhi of the Master must create a reservoir of spiritual energy. The intimate disciples of Maharshi knew about this some thirty years ago. They called it 'The I-Current'. They ascribed to this super-physical power different phenomena that occurred at the Ashram, spontaneous cures of diseases, spiritual illuminations and sudden changes in the direction of their lives. Maharshi himself rarely spoke about any phenomena mentioned by his devotees. It seemed he ignored all this.

It is within the realm of natural law that a powerful spiritual magnetism as created by the Great Rishi could not fail to produce effects on our consciousness when attuned to its mighty radiation.

One day I was seeking a method—apart from the Vichara—to facilitate my attunement with my true Self. At that time the resistance of my mind and emotions barred the way to the silence. Then an idea came: 'Why should I not try to draw upon the Current?' But how? Concentrating all my attention on that problem I intuitively began to repeat, like a mantra, the words: 'I-Current, I-Current', not knowing what made me do it. Immediately a stream of power entered my being, exactly filling the need whose fulfilment I had sought. Now everything was changed. The mind's resistance was swept away. The physical world receded from the screen of my vision like a broken film. Then came the state of consciousness I have described in other chapters.

Later I realized that it was not necessary to use the mystical current only for the above purposes, and that its use in smaller matters could also be helpful. Every disturbance of the mind can be quelled by it. But intuition warns me not to use that reservoir of force too often and without discrimination.

What conditions are necessary to bring one in contact with the 'I-Current'? Knowledge that the current exists; belief in its effectiveness as part of the activity of the Master, and desire for some worthy cause to be served. I never asked my Master about it. It seemed too trivial a thing to speak about, when his work was always performed on a higher level. However, it throws light on the methods by which those who have gone before us have performed their tasks.

The 'I-Current' exists. It constitutes a great source of power on which we can draw to achieve worthy ends. It is the blessed inheritance left to us by the great friend of humanity.

CHAPTER XXI

The Tomb of the Muslim Saint

One day, one of my friends invited me to attend worship in the mosque of Tiruvannamalai. I went and was told the strange story of a North Indian Mohammedan Saint, generally called 'Haji' here. A few days before his death he said to his pupils:

'When I leave my physical form, my Spirit will remain with you. Let everyone, without any difference of creed and social status, come to my grave whenever he may be in need of help. Let him express his need or wish as clearly as he would, were he facing my present visible form. I shall certainly hear his entreaty and shall transmit it to the Most High, Who will fulfil it for the sake of His servant'.

I was told of many cases when such assistance had been granted, irrespective of creed, to Muslim, Hindus and Christians alike. A few days after visiting the caves, on a beautiful evening, I went to see this Haji's tomb. It was in a modest thatched hut. Inside was an old watchman of the mosque who lived nearby, and supplied the incense sticks to be burned day and night at the tomb. It was very simple, oblong in shape, and two small lights were burning on the parapet of the verandah, about a yard and a half deep running round the mud-floored hut. On one side of it could be seen the white walls of the mosque, and from another the sun-scorched fields of the plain.

Silence and peace reigned in this modest shrine. The sun was just setting—a good hour for meditation, and that the place also was most suitable for it, I had in a moment, ample proof.

The psychic atmosphere of India is very different from that of most other countries. One might say that contemplative moods are in the very air. This is easy to understand if we admit that no energy is lost in nature. Millions of human beings, often endowed with extraordinary spiritual powers, with a mighty radiating influence, have from time immemorial been throwing into the atmosphere of India streams of energy generated by their meditations. Also, since the thoughts of many inhabitants are directed towards superphysical aims, all this creates a peculiar magnetism, especially in so-called 'holy' places like the Ashram and its surroundings.

For me, the tomb of the Mohammedan saint proved to be one of these magnetic spots. In a few moments, after having excluded the visible world from my consciousness, I became aware of the Haji's presence. It was like that of a sweet and extremely kind person asking me what were my needs and wishes, and urging me to express them frankly without any shyness or reservation. But on this occasion I had no requests to make, save only the one thought which was always in my mind even in the presence of Maharshi. It is difficult to explain what it was, but for those who know the Indian philosophic terminology, the expression, a wish to enter the 'Stream of Dhyana', would be best. That night this 'stream' carried me farther than I had expected.

*   *   *

During the next weeks I returned several times to this silent shrine, having some entangled and difficult problems to solve. One of them seemed utterly hopeless, for its solution from the physical point of view was impossible. And yet, within three days after my last visit and request for the Haji's help, a happy and unexpected solution came of itself without intervention on my part.

Those of my readers who live on the surface of things, may react to this story in a more comfortable than wise way by saying offhand: 'Oh, it was a mere chance'. Once I asked one such believer in chance to be good enough to explain to me what exactly this word meant to him, and what range of happenings it covered. Alas, I met with sheer vagueness, neither he nor anybody else being willing to give me a logical answer, although they maintained that they knew very well what the word meant, and 'It is so clear, everybody should understand it'. Yet even now I have never heard an adequate explanation. Of course, I do not mind such comments.

CHAPTER XXII

In Sri Aurobindo's Ashram

One day a friend informed me that in a few weeks there would be a Darshan (Audience) of the Master Sri Aurobindo Gosh. It is held twice a year in Pondicherry.

I already knew something about his teachings, explained in various books which have had success in the West. Years ago while in Paris I bought one called *Selected Thoughts and Aphorisms of Sri Aurobindo*. I liked it, at that time, for its bold and clear conceptions, and it was founded on deep wisdom. This occult school in Pondicherry has as its aims the spiritual and cultural unification of the East and West, and the preparation of a group of spiritually enlightened leaders capable of guiding future generations of humanity. As a result laymen often call Sri Aurobindo's Ashram a school of magic.

In order to be admitted to the Darshan, one had to procure a special permit in writing. I was told that it was not too easy to get especially if one had no influence with the Ashram staff. However, I obtained it without any difficulty, and on August 14th I took the train for Pondicherry.

The journey took longer than it should because of custom's formalities on entering the colony, which required two or three hours. On leaving the station, I found the whole town was decorated with French and Indian flags. It was the second anniversary of the Independence of the Indian Republic. The politically astute French Governor, not wishing to offend the Indian population, had the flags of both countries flown on the Government offices and the public eagerly followed his lead, making the small town look very festive. There were also numerous patrols of black French soldiers on bicycles, probably Sengalese from Africa. One of the native sergeants directed me to the Ashram in quite tolerable French.

The Ashram's departments are located in different buildings, its organization being apparently quite effective and smooth, so that long queues for meal and lodging tickets were handled quickly. The Darshan was timed for 3 p.m. At noon I sat in one of the large rooms of a villa where meals were served for the visitors. The lunch of well-cooked vegetarian food was distributed by a sort of self-service, and for those who wished, there was bread and sour milk. The mixture of half-Indian, half-European manners was rather incongruous, for with knives and forks provided, the visitors sat on the floor on clean mats in front of miniature tables. Many Westerners were present among the guests, some being resident in the Ashram itself. The streets close by were full of the latest model cars, and as it was so very hot the thousands of visitors soon emptied the tiny shops of cool drinks. My thirst was not the only one that had to be quenched with luke-warm water. After inspecting the tiny harbour, with its ships anchored by the wooden jetties, I took a short siesta under the trees, but the nearness of the ocean did nothing to cool the temperature.

At 3 p.m., when the gate of the Ashram was opened, the queue of nearly two thousand people, four abreast, seemed to stretch away endlessly. The whole of India and many other countries were represented. After a long wait, I at last came near the home of the Master and the queue entered the hall through alleys and corridors. Pictures of Sri Aurobindo and his collaborator and companion—a French lady, a former actress of great beauty in her younger years—hung on the walls. She is now known as 'Mother' and administers the Ashram with great energy and skill. The Master Aurobindo himself does not handle the business side, but leads a strictly contemplative life. The Mother also manages about two hundred pupils without, it seems, any great effort. Pupils when enrolled usually give all their earthly possessions to the Ashram, which then cares for their needs. Their material worries being removed, every member of this strange community obeys the orders of the Mother. Since each has his work or trade, the Ashram is practically self-supporting, just like a convent or monastery. There is a strict time-table of work, lessons and meditations.

Stepping slowly in the queue I saw notices on the walls telling us that the most appropriate attitude is one of meditation and silence. Incidentally, it was said that the Mother was clairvoyant and that a few of the more critically-minded visitors were sometimes sent away without being allowed to see the Master.

Now as we approached the room, we saw Sri Aurobindo and the Mother seated in the wide doorway; on the right and left were large boxes for flowers and gifts. At last I saw the strange couple. The queue moved slowly, so I could observe them at my leisure. They sat in deep concentration without any movement. Sri Aurobindo was a well-built man with white hair, his face more like that of a European than an Indian. The broad forehead suggested great intelligence, while the piercing eyes looked into space. I had an overwhelming impression of powerful mental forces vibrating round the couple. The face of the Mother was partly covered by a veil attached to her sari. I could not see her eyes. The same intensive concentration was expressed by her whole figure. She looked even older than the Master himself, who was then about 74 years, as one of the inmates of the Ashram informed me. When I was only a dozen feet away, I had a strange feeling in my throat and neck as if they were stiff and paralysed. Certainly at that moment I could not have spoken a word or made any movement other than stepping slowly in the queue. But my mind was working as clearly as usual, for I thought of an astral protecting sphere with which some occultists cover themselves. I am not at all susceptible to so-called hypnotic suggestion and could never be hypnotized. There was no clouding of my consciousness, but it seemed as if my physical body was bound by an invisible force. The strange feeling continued until I had passed another dozen or so steps away from the pair. Then everything was restored to normal and I regained the ability to speak if I wished, for complete silence reigned as the line passed the Master and Mother.

That was all I felt in the presence of Sri Aurobindo. There was no trace of that sublime spiritual atmosphere felt in the presence of

Sri Maharshi, or of that wonderful inner contact and living inspiration which radiate from the Rishi. It is not my intention to make
comparisons, for I spoke with some disciples who looked upon
their Master Aurobindo with great veneration and love, and I have
no doubt about the beneficial influence they felt at his feet. But
each type of man needs his own Master and this one was not mine.
That is all I can say.

Later I visited the well-stocked book-shop of the Ashram, and
its library, and was somewhat astonished to find, besides well-
known works of the Master himself, many former friends known
to me in the past—popular works on Western and Eastern occultism and philosophy and on the development of the hidden powers
in man. They were mostly in French and English, and there were
textbooks about concentration and meditation, and even on
hypnotism. But now all these fascinating things had lost their
charm for me. I realized that I was no longer interested in anything
unconnected with my Path. It seemed as if knowledge of the
Direct Path as shown by my Master subconsciously excluded all
else. It meant that the desires of the mind, which is always eager to
investigate everything, had begin to disappear. Vasanas—to a
certain degree—had lost their power over me. Now I understood
from whence came this peace of mind, I had sought for so many
years. This comparison of my past and present was the last of its
kind and was perhaps the only profit I gained from my visit to
Pondicherry.

In the evening I took part in the meditations and worship performed in the large hall of the Ashram. Everything proceeded
smoothly and harmoniously and was full of deep symbolical meaning. Scores of white-robed disciples and visitors filled the vast
room. Then the Master appeared with the Mother for a short time.
Full of dignity and powerful concentration, his face showed
solemnity and inspiration. But in spite of all this my real being
was absent hundreds of miles to the West, in a temple built of grey
Indian granite—for there, seen through tiny streams of violet
incense, amidst a few disciples and devotees sat the One, nearing

the end of his earthly days, to whom a gracious Providence had shown me the way in this fateful period of my life. One who kindles and sheds around an invisible mystical light, reviving within us the memory of the same light hidden in the depths of our own hearts.

Beyond all theories and teachings of the mind is this light. We who sat before the Sage of Arunachala derive from *it* help for every need. From this light can be drawn all knowledge that can be expressed in the language of the mind. This light is the source of all initiation, and no scripture can be properly understood without *it*, and no real Peace attained. For *it* is the Centre, and from *it* arise all rays which pierce the darkness of the material world.

There did not appear to be any ill-feeling on the part of the disciples of Sri Aurobindo towards the 'Jungle Ashram' as the abode of Sri Maharshi was sometimes called. Moreover many pupils from Pondicherry visited Tiruvannamalai and sat at the feet of the Great Rishi and had talks with him.

These facts are noted in dialogues recorded in the diaries of some inmates of the Ashram and some valuable articles were contributed by two pupils of Sri Aurobindo to the book *The Golden Jubilee Souvenir*, published by the Ashram of Sri Maharshi on the occasion of his completion of fifty years spent at the foot of Arunachala.

★   ★   ★

At last Maharshi returned to the temple hall, and it was possible to resume meditation in his presence.

CHAPTER XXIII

The Darshan Resumed

It is the morning meditation. The temple hall is full. I see many new faces, not only Indian, but from other lands as well. In this peculiar atmospbere of India it is easy to understand the feelings of those gathered around the departing Saint. I almost venture to say that it would not be difficult to 'see' the thoughts of every single person in the hall. But this kind of curiosity or experiment has no place in this sacred abode. It would be a sacrilege.

One thing is clear: we take farewell of the Maharshi, each one according to his own capacity. The form of it does not matter. We are all united at the feet of the Master in adoration and—in Silence.

Near me, I see an elderly European gentleman, dressed only in a shirt and navy-blue shorts, with a rosary round his neck. He has probably spent a long time in India, for his skin is uniformly brownish in hue. Short grey hair and moustache adorn a thin and somewhat sad face. He is looking at the Master with a certain immobility as if trying to engrave Maharshi's features on his mind forever. He seems to be aware that it is the last time that he will be able to contemplate the Guru's countenance. He left after two days and I have not seen him since. During our common meals, he sat in the farthest corner of the hall, had his own spoon, fork and plates, took only a few dishes, and had milk specially served for him, as it had been for me.

Yogi Ramiah, immovable in contemplation, with a face as if cut from granite, is sitting at his Master's feet, surrounded by Brahmins of the Ashram staff.

An elderly lady, just opposite me, is gazing intently at Maharshi with an expression of boundless devotion, but also of despair and a kind of inner revolt, as if she is unable to accept the certainty that soon she will no longer see him in his earthly form.

And Maharshi? After this new operation, he is thinner than ever; the features seem to be transparent, the colour of his face more fair, as if there were nothing earthly about him. A statue, an abstraction incarnate, if this expression can convey any meaning. No, it is the spirit, which, from the sphere of matter, returns to its own realm, and is only in a very loose and subtle way in touch with what we see as the physical body of the Saint.

His peace is permeating everything all round us. There are no more unsolved problems, no unfulfilled desires, no movements in my consciousness. It is now clear that there is no need of thinking as it seemed before—for thinking is an unnecssary, purposeless thing.

What is it that concerns me now? What is happening to me?

Where is that man who had a name, and many thoughts? All this now seems so far from—'Me'. Oh, if I could only hold this state at any cost, and not return to the world of shadows and illusions! If I could only remain in this silence wherein there is no 'I' and 'you', no time, no space!

The *light* is now pouring out in such abundance that everything is inundated by It. The open eyes see nothing but *light*.

I know that this form, now so foreign to me, seems not to breathe any more. Would its breath disturb the peace of eternity? I do not know.

In this light the boundaries of the 'past' and the 'future' are vanishing, both are now like open plains. No, it is not true, for the momentary awe before the opening of the great gate now gives way to the happiness of awareness that time does not exist any more. Like a lightning flash come to my memory, the words of the Revelation of St. John: ' . . . *that there should be time no longer*'.

Yes, I now realize that true life is independent of time, and that if we are still living in time, it is not real life. Resurrection, that unfathomable mystery, becomes a realized truth, *here* in this *invisible light*.

Everything is adjusted, united, corresponding each to the other in full harmony. Only words fail to express what one sees. Mere fragments remain in the brain, which serves as a medium to put these bits together and transform them into coherent thoughts and words. But—then we are no more 'there'.

*   *   *

How long this new state lasts I do not know, for '*there*' it can be measured neither in hours, nor even in seconds of time. In this state there is no thought about it all, and the intuitional certainty that as soon as I allow even one thought to enter my mind, I shall fall back '*here*', where I do not want to return, helps me to stay in this contemplation. But afterwards, I am unable to remember this state clearly; probably contact with the mind was completely severed, so that no bridge remained.

*   *   *

I now find myself sitting by one of the columns in the hall and looking almost with wonder at everything around me. My first thought is : 'Shall I be able to repeat this plunge into silence again ? Shall I not forget the path which leads to that land ?' But the mind has not yet recovered its usual alertness, and I am not at all anxious to return to it. The blissful state of inner silence and peace still continues. Then from the violet smoke of the incense Maharshi's face emerges before my eyes. The same motionless gaze looks into the vast beyond, but with one difference : it seems that at the same time, he is looking into my inner being as well and seeing what I experienced a moment ago. Yes, I am certain that he knows all of it. Who else could see if not Maharshi ? I may have been a guest for a moment, in the *land where he permanently dwells*.

Now a mute but intense prayer flashes out of my whole being : 'Oh, take me *there* ! Do allow me to live for ever in that blessed Land ! I do not care any more for this illusory world. I shall gladly step through the gate of death if such be the condition'.

I see that he is now definitely looking at me and the answer is ready in his luminous eyes. The unreasonable outburst is stilled. I am now reconciled with what is unavoidable. I know that all is and must be for the best. Everything will come in due time, just as time is needed for the ripening of a fruit, for the change of a chrysalis into a butterfly.

*   *
*

The sound of the gong is heard. Everyone stands up when Maharshi, with the assistance of his attendants, gets up and goes towards the door. It is the hour of the noon meal.

Maharshi is always insistent on perfect equality on the physical plane. One of its expressions is his care about a perfectly equal distribution of food. Several times I have witnessed his personal intervention when the share of one or two among the numerous guests seemed to him to be smaller than that of the others. One morning when we found on our leaves, besides the usual rice-cakes, some fruit—a banana, a few pieces of orange and apple—the Sage broke his silence, habitual during meals, and said a few words to the serving Brahmin in an almost severe tone. Here I saw what a tremendous significance the slightest hint of the Master has for all who are near him as inmates of the Ashram. The poor Brahmin rushed to my leaf, begged me to excuse him and, shy as he was, seized it with all its contents and took it to show to the Maharshi. At first I could not understand what it all meant, but I soon realized that the Sage was counting the fruit on my leaf and comparing the number with those on his own. As soon as he saw that the quantity was the same, he addressed the serving Brahmin more graciously, making a gesture in my direction. The man answered a few words visibly comforted to have justified himself before the highest tribunal, and then he brought back my breakfast.

To those who have not witnessed this little scene and have not known the Master personally, it might seem insignificant or even naïve. But Maharshi knows human hearts with all their weaknesses and imperfections. That is why the remedies which he administers, when he judges it proper, never fail in their results. What could be more encouraging and comforting than to see such a simple friendly gesture on the part of a spiritual giant like him? I understood only later the meaning of it all.

In spite of the usual unvarying, extremely kind and friendly attitude of the Saint, one is rather shy in his presence, especially in the beginning, and this may become a hindrance to one's inner approach. Our intuition whispers to us the tremendous difference in the levels between ourselves and him.

But the Maharshi discards this unbecoming and egocentric attitude without words, showing by his own example what should be our behaviour with others.

CHAPTER XXIV

Initiations

When in the presence of the Master our mind ceases to be a hindrance to seeing reality, there comes the dawn of a new intuitional understanding of all spiritual teaching given in the far-off 'past', as well as in our own days by those who Themselves have realized the truth.

I notice that, unexpectedly for myself, questions and problems which some time ago were unintelligible or postponed for later solution have solved themselves. First of all, the wish to 'reconcile' these teachings intellectually has disappeared. I now see how shallow and futile is such a wish to judge and compare systems and their particular goals, given in different times and to different races of humanity. It was my mania some time ago. I wanted to find at any cost some definite and comfortable synthesis, and cling to it for my own satisfaction. Now I see that it leads nowhere, that it is a sheer waste of time and a wandering in darkness, for such an objective synthesis cannot exist. On the other hand I see that there are as many paths as there are different consciousnesses manifested in one or another form of existent life. A friend once expressed the opinion that there are many ways of approaching the one being, and that every lesson ultimately leads to truth. I now see the basic tragic misunderstanding. *What* is it that we have to *know*? Is it the innumerable varieties of material forms, or our individual reactions to them? It is clear that such a process of acquiring knowledge never finds fulfilment; as each manifested form corresponds to some thought, so each thought is accompanied by a new form, another subject for our examination and our 'knowledge'.

Why cannot people understand this simple truth? There is not, nor can there be, any hope of acquiring objective knowledge about all the forms of existence, and there can be no end to such an endeavour. The goal would recede further and further, and no one would ever see its end. Maharshi says:

'To try to know the forms which exist in time and space would be as nonsensical as for a man, who has just been shaved or had his hair cut, to brood over the fate of each of these hairs'.

They will be thrown into a dust-bin or burned. In either case there will be no further contact between them and their original owner. The past is also an illusion of the transient imagination; it can never return, nor repeat its meaning for those who were once its actors. In this fact we discover why and how human beings are apt to add so much to the bitterness and suffering of their lives. They for ever chew over the cud of past experiences, which do not exist any more, thus missing the meaning of the *Now*. They live in the past instead of plunging into the present and living it to the full. Self-knowledge or *realization* stops these aimless errings. I know that time and space do not exist for the Sage who I am now facing, and I see in this fact a joyous hope for myself. This is an initiation.

I know the life of the Maharshi in all its details, as given by his nearest followers in their various writings. While the young Ramana, still at home with his parents, was reading the history of the sixty-three saints of the Saivite cult, there arose spontaneously within his heart a firm determination to become one of them. Similarly when one is looking at Maharshi, the only desire left in our hearts is to become like him. A power which cannot be compared with anything in the world compels us to see our highest and final goal in uniting with the consciousness of the Sage. And for one moment this vision becomes reality. For silence is one and all-embracing. All life is merged in It, and everything that is beyond this life—the unchangeable and infinitely blissful, with no qualities and therefore, with no limitations.

The words of one of the less-known Western mystics are really true, when he says that God and truth are so simple, and at the same time so dazzling, that if He would manifest Himself in all His shining splendour, *no planet could stand it, but would instantly be turned to ashes*. It may be an allegory, but I know that it contains a mystic truth. It is an initiation.

Here, at the feet of the Sage, I have made peace with the world. It has ceased to be an alien giant, incomprehensible in all its endless intricacies. And those whom I see as men no longer appear as separate and foreign beings, for the same innermost and unchanging principle which resides in me also dwells in all my brethren. This feeling is awakened by practising Maharshi's instruction : 'When you meet someone think deeply : It is God who dwells in this body'.

Then comes initiation for ever.

CHAPTER XXV

A Musical Performance in the Temple Hall

Today I noticed, near to the column opposite Maharshi's couch, two wooden boxes covered with coloured Indian rugs. Two men dressed in North Indian fashion were sitting near them. The librarian of the Ashram, an elderly Brahmin, with whom I had long conversations during his office hours in the Library, informed me that in the afternoon there was to be a recital of religious music in the presence of Maharshi, and that the newcomers were well-known artists who would play on small harmoniums of their own construction. The temple hall was full that afternoon, as rarely happened. The musicians, after the usual prostration before the Sage, began their programme. One led on a larger instrument, giving the melody, and the other accompanied him. It was a strange mixture of classical motifs with purely Eastern interpolations, somewhat like the songs which were sung during the night meditation by the pupils of the Master.

Maharshi was sitting as usual in a kind of deep concentration on some infinitely distant subject and did not appear to be listening very attentively to the music. After about an hour the musicians concluded their recital, once more prostrated before Maharshi, and then sat quietly among the other devotees. I was keenly interested as to the manner in which they played their harmoniums. The first hardly seemed to touch the keys, while his companion appeared to move his fingers above the box, which apparently did not have any keys at all, at any rate I did not see any from the position where I was sitting. I had once heard about an electric harmonium, which emitted sound as the musician's fingers approached it, his way of moving them and their distance from the instrument determining the tones which came forth. Is it possible that these Indian artists had used such an instrument? But I had not noticed any wires linking their boxes with the power points in the hall, whereby electricity could have been obtained.

After the night meditation, I was accosted at the door by one of the young attendants, who informed me that there was to be a film show after supper. He asked me to invite some of the other Europeans and Americans staying in the neighbourhood. At about 8 p.m. the hall was full of activity. In one of the corners a screen was placed; in another was a small projector; several technicians were at work.

My Western friends came early. I found a good place on a window-sill for myself and a Bombay friend, Miss Nalini, with whom I had many talks during her stay near the Ashram. A young girl of fifteen or sixteen, the daughter of a rich aristocratic family from Calcutta, also joined us.

I noticed the presence of the official hierarchy of the town of Tiruvannamalai—the Superintendent of Police, a giant in khaki uniform, the District Medical Officer, and several advocates and Judges of the local Courts.

After some adjustments the show began. The films were concerned with Maharshi's life, and showed him in many different scenes—climbing the sacred hill of Arunachala, walking in the Ashram compound, or taking part in some of its festivities. The films, chiefly coloured, were quite good, the figure of the Saint being in natural and vivid colours. I recognized many of the people surrounding him, such as the same indispensable Superintendent of Police and some of the Brahmins of the Ashram staff. A group of Indian Scouts were also seen taking meals in the Maharshi's presence. An American lady, a fervent admirer of the Sage, was walking just behind him in several of the films.

Maharshi gazed at the show with an almost imperceptible, kind little smile on his habitually serious face. And I could not help but think: 'So the figure of the Saint has already been "immortalized" for future generations. But this will never compensate for his living presence, this blessing that we now have with us for so short a time'.

CHAPTER XXVI

Apart from the Mind

'Therefore the *manas* is the cause of the bondage of this individual and also of its liberation. The manas when stained by passion is the cause of bondage, and of liberation when pure, devoid of passion and ignorance'.

Sankaracharya, *Viveka-Chudamani*, Verse 176

Around the Ashram's temple is a broad terrace of concrete and stone. After 9 p.m. life in the big compound is almost still, and the temple itself is darkened. Maharshi sleeps in the hall, which is separated from the temple proper by a massive gate of iron grid, artistically fashioned in Indian style. Besides the Master, there are always one or two attendants who never leave him, and are ready to give any service required. This is most necessary now that his health is so precarious.

Some nights, when the moon sheds its light over the silent paths, I come here from my room and sit quietly on the clean-swept terrace. Still figures of some native country visitors recline asleep on the sandy area before the dining-hall, and the Ashram's pool lies peacefully before me.

I find the spot appropriate for meditation. Perhaps the awareness of the Master's presence only a few dozen yards away, adds solemnity to my thoughts. Among many things learned at his feet, there is one of overwhelming importance, which I wish to enlarge on here.

Four years ago, when I read Paul Brunton's account of an ecstatic state of consciousness which he experienced in the presence of the Great Rishi, describing it as being apart from the thinking mind, it was rather an enigma to me. How could one be apart and independent of his own mentality?

Now I have proved it possible by experience.

It was said earlier, that after my arrival at the Ashram I stopped all my previous exercises. This was done because I felt with utter certainty that the precious time spent here with my Master should be more wisely used. Exercises could be performed later, if need be. But here and now, I must take the opportunity of learning what might otherwise be impossible.

After the fateful experience described in Chapter XXIII, I realized that I could be separated from my thinking apparatus, and that my consciousness or awareness of being, was far from being obliterated. Life flowed on without hindrance, though the mind was without thought. I now knew that the 'I-Current' is independent of thought, and yet every process of thought is produced from It.

This is one of the highest initiations through which one passes when in the presence of the Master.

Years ago, after long, tedious instruction that the mind must be subdued before any ray of light can reach one, I began my endless exercises in that direction, with feelings of pain and uncertainty. Now I see why. The region beyond mind was, for me at that time, an unexplored land—an emptiness. Then I was completely devoid of this self-conscious power, the awareness of which was born with the mysterious help of Maharshi. The former method of using the mind was like the dangerous situation of a man in charge of an electric motor which is running hot, and who does not know where to find the switch to stop it. Can the average man stop his thinking machine when he wishes? Does a man use a machine which he is unable to control? What is humanity doing?

The mind—that most subtle and essential power which we have before we discover our true Self—remains uncontrolled and its switch unknown. It leads us where it will, often down blind alleys and bypaths. But our true Self knows all. The first rays of Its light gave me control of that mysterious 'switch'. Now doubt and uncertainty have gone.

*   *   *

Now my eyes are open and I see the silvery water of the Ashram's pool, while above, white clouds drift across the sky,

H

with the moon rising between them. My outer ears hear the muffled cries of far-off owls, but all this is outside my consciousness. I am aware that my physical self is in contact with the outer world, but within, the true 'I' reigns in stillness. I would not accept all the wealth of the universe for this stillness. I know that it is the foundation which will not be lost when the world of the senses crumbles. This stillness has no desires. It is independent of all. When It takes the foreground of my consciousness, all that I once thought of as 'myself', vanishes. One cannot see 'It' for the simple reason that in that state nothing but *it* exists.

The words 'diving' and 'merging', often used in attempting to describe this state, are unsuitable, for they suggest something separate, and an entering into something unknown. The experience itself is quite different. One then is this stillness and nothing else. One is then stripped of all veils and only the essence remains.

*   *   *

A strange condition begins to develop in me. I look on the Mouni Sadhu as on an object, and this outer shell is not by any means the most important: he sits and breathes, and blood circulates in his veins. I see many thoughts around the mind—like a swarm of bees trying to enter their hive—but the stillness, the silence forbids invasion.

I know that the next stage of consciousness will bring me to the vanishing of this visible world. Some months ago, this vanishing invariably brought me a gap in the awareness of the Life flowing in me. But now it is different. I know that I cannot lose the consciousness of this 'I-Current' in me any more.

Everything can and will pass but *I am*! Nameless, formless, the only onlooker—*I am*—I exist.

Persistence in this state is effortless, but strangely enough I know that for my visible counterpart, there is great effort, and most of all for my mind-brain. I feel that it is literally straining under the vibratory power of these new and hitherto unknown currents of consciousness. Now I realize why I cannot remain for ever in them. My outer form, and especially the brain, cannot yet bear it.

So I must return from this realm of silence. But awareness of *it*, though dim and imperfect, still remains through that 'return'.

The awareness of this current is the power which makes it possible for these experiences beyond the mind to be transmitted and expressed on paper. The fact is hard to convey, but the knowledge that the mind is not *me*, is the very source of this ability. Put simply, if I can order my involuntary thinking to stop, and can see the accomplished fact, then, he who gives the order is *me*. The equation is solved. The mysterious unknown quantity 'X' is found.

During the following nights I tried to find Myself while in the state of physical sleep. As I presumed, it was far more difficult than when I attempted it while awake; for then I could control the mind as independent of the physical body and brain. In sleep my physical counterpart is in a different condition, which has not yet been brought under discipline. At the time I could not find any hint as to how the thing was to be accomplished. But sometimes on awakening, I remember that I must have had a certain kind of awareness of 'I' while asleep. Intuition—the soundless voice—whispers that the solution will come in due course. So there is no need to hasten it prematurely.

★   ★   ★

The presence of the Master is now felt even when I cannot see him—when I am away from the hall. How can this be? The process of seeking while the mind is still, conveys to me the Truth, which I see as if in a flash of light.

The Master is not the body which I see every day on the couch in the temple. He is this stillness—the silence itself, in which I realize myself. This knowledge immediately brings me peace, for it is not knowledge of the mind, it is truth itself.

A description of truth cannot help us. It must be lived and experienced. That is why I lost all interest in books written by those who themselves have not experienced truth, and have only built theories based on mental conceptions. To me, they are lifeless and useless.

Truth is life. They are never separated. It is clear to me that where there is no life, there cannot be truth. So I must say, good-bye to my old companions—books—for they cannot help me any more. A few, which contain real experience, are always in my memory. They confirm what I have now experienced, and in gratitude to them, I quote from them in my diary. They helped me at appropriate times and they may do the same for the reader.

At about midnight I return to my room, an Indian cat is waiting for me on the dark paths of the Ashram's compound. I regularly give her food, mostly rice and milk, and stroke her short white-grey fur. Apparently I am the only one to whom the half-wild little animal allows such intimacy: she runs away from others.

In gratitude she carefully inspects my room and devours the unwelcome big red spiders which often pay their respects to me at night. So we are good friends.

CHAPTER XXVII

Stray Leaves

The following pages reflect different moods and states of mind experienced by me during my stay in the Ashram. Reading them now, through the perspective of almost one year, I see the changes which were, and still are taking place in the being called 'me'. I have put these fragments together into one chapter, as they are mostly short and of a fleeting, sporadic character.

My whole attitude towards the world and human beings changed greatly, as I have mentioned before, but these modifications took place spontaneously and almost unconsciously. I first noticed that my behaviour under certain conditions had formerly been quite different, and that now those very situations appeared to me in quite another light. The desire for synthesis had now become the dominant note of my moods; desire to attain such a state of consciousness as would enable me to see everything in its true light, with no personal colouring. I felt that such a level exists and I wanted to find it at any cost. I also *knew* that it would not be found in the realm of mental theories, for I had changed those many times during the long years of my search. This search for a synthesis would probably be painful and accompanied by an intense inner conflict if experienced anywhere other than in the Ashram; the presence of the Saint puts an end to all intellectual stunts. Here one's roots simply grow into truth.

Religious prejudices and occult theories likewise dropped away of themselves. The field of vision around the Self cleared up. Even quite recently, from old habits, when I turned my thoughts to the Christ I excluded Siva. In my meditation on the '*Self*' there was no place for Buddha. After that came a period when the figure of Maharshi replaced all that could be known by the critical mind. This state lasted several weeks and it was a time of carefree peace.

It was probably a necessary preparation for more abstract and subtle experiences.

After this period was over, I noticed that many mental barriers and hindrances were dissolved in a new state where no contradiction existed. It was during this time that I paid my visits to the tomb of the Mohammedan Saint at the foot of Arunachala hill and learned that there, as well as here, one finds the same possibilities and assistance in escaping from the bondage of one's annoying personality.

The hue of the first mood which is an introduction, as it were, to further experiences, may be somewhat different, but as soon as the chain of thoughts is broken, the identity is felt. That is why Maharshi repeats that all paths, if properly understood, lead to the same goal.

What can be brought back from the land of silence to be expressed in words? How can one possibly convey all the modifications which take place in the moods of the experiencer? For instance, one suddenly feels a certainty of the unity of all existence and in that light the fear of death appears to be absurd. This kind of dissolution into or identification with the *whole* is accompanied by a great sense of bliss which is akin to resurrection.

I immediately know that the only way to life is to let go of the illusion of a separate existence in the physical or any other form. I know that all the changes which constitute the basic element of life—rather of consciousness limited and enclosed in form—are not real but illusory and hence they must be accompanied by suffering which is a kind of antidote to the 'strong and intoxicating wine of Maya' (Matter).

This brings an unshakable conviction that all activity, if performed with attachment, forges new chains of existence in forms, and hence new waves of suffering. That there is nothing absolutely 'necessary', and that all the anxieties concerning the 'future of humanity' or its particular races and nations are simply a waste of energy and that our foremost task is to know our own little world, and to find our own real Self. Of course, we can be tools in the great plan which is realized by the Most High according to His own will and design, but to think that *we* are performing any action is a sheer illusion. One remarks however, that the word 'we' denotes our *personality*, and that it means the complex bundle of form, mind, name and so on. When we approach the *real Self* we see that we are *one* with the *Creator*.

But—how many steps and stages are there on this path, how many 'initiations' have we to pass through?

CHAPTER XXVIII

The Eyes of Maharshi

During the Darshan in the hall, there is usually no one between me and Maharshi's couch, which means that I can contemplate his eyes with no obstacles between, their gaze being generally turned in my direction, and usually looking straight ahead. At first I lacked the courage to look intently into the face of the Sage. Perhaps this shyness was the last vestige of those worldly habits which do not permit a well-behaved person to gaze insistently into the eyes of another. There may also have been another reason : my intuition was whispering that those eyes saw infinitely farther than ordinary human eyes, which meant that the whole content of my being was wide open before their gaze. Some time was needed to get rid of this feeling of shyness, which in the Roman Catholic world makes confession before a priest so difficult for some people.

But the effort had to be made, and in a few weeks all obstacles disappeared and a mute, yet a thousandfold more efficacious 'confession' became a daily practice in my inner contact with Maharshi. I had to learn 'utter frankness', for without this quality there cannot be any direct spiritual approach to the Master.

The eyes of Maharshi always seem to be the same, for I cannot see in them any modification of expression due to emotion or thought. But that does not mean that they are devoid of the shining glow of life ! On the contrary, light and life are constantly flowing through them with a majesty and intensity unimaginable to those who have not seen them. The large dark pupils are always full of resplendent light. Even in his photographs this extraordinary intensity of light in his eyes is noted by every careful observer, even though he may not know the one they represent.

A stream of peace, powerful yet sweet, flows from these eyes. They glow with a perfect understanding of all the weaknesses, defects and inner difficulties of those who look into them. Personally I have also noticed in them a slight, almost imperceptible, smile of indulgence for the whole surrounding world and all of us here, who are representatives of the 'great illusion'. And when I look almost by chance into the eyes of some of the people in the hall, I see that they do not reflect in the slightest degree, even a fragment of the light which is shining through Maharshi's eyes. In comparison they seem to be almost lifeless, and I am not able to get rid of this impression—at least for the moment I am unable to control it—though I know that making such comparisons is wrong, and that I should not pass judgment on others. Everyone is just what he is able to be, neither more nor less, and life is the same in each one of us. Yet, although I accept the truth of it in theory, I cannot help feeling this difference whenever I look into the eyes of the Saint and then happen to gaze into those of others. This thought, although wrong and unjust, slips into my mind, as it were and abides there until I invite it to leave by means of the well-known 'Self-Inquiry' or 'Vichara'.

The Highest manifests Himself in everything and every living being, however low its level may seem to us. He is present in the plant and in the insect, in the snake, in the animal and in man. The difference is only in the degree and perfection of His manifestation. It is obvious that we are able to perceive only an infinitesimal part of the manifested absolute; the higher forms of His revelation are beyond the reach of our limited consciousness. And yet there must be something just on this last boundary of our perceptive faculties, which reflects in all perfection the gaze of God.

A strange new and powerful current awakens in my consciousness. It is with a kind of expectation that I am trying to hold all my attention above the ocean of changing thoughts. I seem to hear a whisper: 'Persevere and you will find the answer'. Suddenly light comes, It is like a lightning flash of tremendous power. I am dazzled, terrified, for a moment in the face of the reality seen.

Of course, there is no hope of being able to convey this vision to others in words. But now I am entitled to say:

'*I know who looks through Maharshi's eyes*'.

CHAPTER XXIX

'Asperges me hyssopo . . .'

'Asperges me hyssopo—mundabor.
Lavabis me aqua—et super nivem dealbabor'
'Sprinkle me with hyssop and I shall be clean,
Wash me with water and I shall be whiter than snow'.

For thirty years Maharshi has held his 'Office', and performed his mission here in this quiet little-known corner of India, not through preaching and lecturing about spiritual truth, which he has realized to such an amazing degree, but by his very presence. Like a lofty beacon whose beams point the way to safe harbour for all on the high seas who are searching for a haven, so this great Rishi of India sheds light on those who have eyes to see and ears to hear.

Day after day, year after year, he is here in the Ashram and always approachable for all people during the greater part of the day, full of silence and peace, such as are possessed only by those who have attained the highest spiritual achievement.

These thoughts rush through my mind like a stream from a source far away in the high mountains unknown to me. I do not try to discover those heights as I would probably have tried to do some time ago.

Why should a man seek light when he is facing its very source . This light permeates our being through and through to give us an insight into all the mistakes, and imperfections of our 'ego', our little insignificant personality. The presence of the source makes it possible for the rays to penetrate our being naturally and most infallibly *from within*, as it were, and not *from without*. So there is no fear of an *imposition*, or suggestion of anything from outside. Then begins the slow process of purification, arising out of the contemplation of the *living example*.

I notice that some of my blunders and 'sins' which seemed to be deeply rooted during the years of my former life, have now become anachronisms, in fact impossibilities. Some inner moods, formerly rather frequent and provoking much suffering and conflict, are now dissolved like a distant mist. And the uncertainty, so common to all human beings—as a matter of fact their constant companion from the cradle to the grave—an uncertainty covered up by all kinds of theories, religious practices, and the membership of different organizations founded and guided by men as blind as they themselves, is slowly disappearing from my consciousness and giving way to the dawn of a new life.

Sitting every day, as long as I can, at the feet of the Sage, I have neither the time nor desire for a careful analysis of the changes taking place in my being. I know that whatever is happening should be so. I also know that I have to struggle with all the obstacles imposed by the unreal world, which seem to pull me back to roads I have left and to lead me astray. But all in vain. When once we clearly realize that these were by-ways there cannot be any return to them. My personality, of course, is not quite happy about it all, for it has to keep silent during these hours over which it was formerly an all-powerful ruler.

The thought of 'salvation', so often dimming the sight of those who seek a selfish 'heaven', now seems ridiculous. The real 'salvation' will come when the very object seeking salvation disappears.

The activity of the perverse mental poison manifesting itself in a comparison of oneself to others is also dying out. And the real meaning of the words of all great teachers of humanity from time immemorial, and repeated in many eras and in different forms, seems to open before my understanding.

Why cannot the world perceive this one and the same Essence of Their teachings? Why does it give its narrow interpretation to Their words, to suit its own convenience and to avoid all effort?

Once Maharshi, when asked 'What is the primordial sin' spoken of by one of the great religions of the world, answered: '*It is the illusion of a separate personal existence*'.

That is indeed the source and root of all blunders and sufferings.

In truth what can be expected from withdrawing into a narrow circle of selfish personal life? Only an unavoidable destruction of the man who is himself putting a sword into the hands of death, whose duty is to annihilate that which really has never been more than nothingness.

I see that the writing of these fragments of my meditations takes far more time than my consciousness needed to realize them during the time of the actual experience. It is somewhat similar to a film actually, in which only seconds and minutes are needed to take individual scenes and events, while it requires an hour or so to contemplate the completed product. My next thought is: 'Why look at the film at all?'

*　　*　　*

This evening, when leaving the hall after meditation, I stopped on the steps of the temple facing the drive leading out of the Ashram compound to the highroad. In the infinite spaces of the starry sky innumerable universes are scattered, looking down on our Earth, always the same, always distant and yet now so near. These immensities, these infinities of space, no longer evoke in me feelings of nothingness as they did when I believed in the reality of their existence. It was an illusion which is created when we look at everything from the point of view of our own impermanent physical form. But when the belief in the reality of our body vanishes, the whole film of the Cosmos appears to be nothing more than it really is:

A play of light and shadow.

CHAPTER XXX

Arunachala by Night

To-night after meditation in the hall, I went to the hill and sat on a rock which had probably rolled down from the higher parts of Siva's mountain to the bed of the stream, which during the rainy season rushes behind the Ashram's compound. The night was calm and hot, and in the east rain clouds were gathering, clouds from the ocean that were slowly moving towards Tiruvannamalai.

The outlines of Arunachala peak were clear cut and sharp against the sky. The lower, massive body of the hill remained invisible, wrapped in the darkness of night. I have never failed to feel the strange magnetic influence of Arunachala even in its visible form. At first I could not rationally explain what relation there could be between Maharshi and the hill, for I knew that the Sage was far beyond all special beliefs, and that he regarded the whole world as an illusion and a play of our physical senses. And yet it was undeniable that even in his books he mentions Arunachala with the highest reverence and love. It is mysterious, at least for those who have not fathomed the symbolism of this strange South Indian hill.

In this quiet night meditation I decided to use the newly-discovered method of perceiving that which is imperceptible to the ordinary mental faculties. This method consists in a preliminary purification of the mind of all thoughts, leaving only the intention of getting into touch from 'within', as it were, with the desired object of cognition. Afterwards what is translatable into the language of the mind is transmitted to it. In other words, intuition has to provide light from a source which the mind cannot reach.

The powerful magnetism of Arunachala makes the whole process easier. As soon as I plunged into meditation, discarding all objects from my sight, I began to see that for which I had been searching.

First of all became clear the well-known occult law that—
'Everything has its corresponding form of manifestation in different worlds'. Hence that which is the spiritual essence of Arunachala can have its reflection on the physical plane, just as that
which constitutes the real man has its corresponding counterpart
on the visible plane in this form which is called 'man' only through
illusion. Obviously something had to be created on this earth for
the sake of earthly beings, to remind them of their immortal heri-
tage in the only real sphere, that of the Spirit. Hindus, according
to their religious conceptions call 'That' the 'Form of Siva', and so
on. They say that in remotest times, when humanity was beginning
its existence on our globe, Siva himself appeared on the summit of
Arunachala as a column of living fire. Why should I not accept
this symbol as meaning that spirit-life in time bursts forth from
the mortal vehicle where it has been hidden?

I have always seen the paramount need for resurrection. So the
symbol of this hill, this mass of immovable physical matter,
whose peak throws forth into heaven a flash of fire, reveals to me
its real meaning. To me, as to many others, Arunachala was, and
is, a sign-post on the Path.

Later on, I also devoted a good deal of time to an attempt to
understand what Maharshi himself expressed in his short and con-
cise style about the qualities of Arunachala. Most interesting was
his assertion that even the mental image of the sacred hill is enough
to stop the fatal round of endless thoughts which makes our
approach to truth and realization impossible. That same night, I
proved by experience that this *was right*.

Maharshi also said: '*Arunachala destroys attachment to worldly
things, that is to the objects of physical illusion*'. This I proved later,
when I found that every time Arunachala was mentioned or described by those who regarded it as their beacon, I felt this worldly
illusion disappearing from my thoughts, falling into the shadows
of unreality, which is their true source.

I also soon understood that it is not wise to accept only those
things which are translatable into the language of the mind. Every

man in order to supplement the stock of physical energy in his body, thus enabling it to rebuild its worn-out particles, and assure its growth and development, must take the proper amount and quality of food, but it is not necessary for him to remember the chemical content of each morsel he swallows. Even science has asserted that the more natural is the process of eating, and the more unconscious and without any interference from the mind, the better it is for our body.

If Arunachala can be a great help, a powerful impulse in my spiritual progress, what does it matter if I am unable to get a clear analysis of the process? The most important ones in the Universe as well as in our own consciousness take place in a natural and simple way. Is it not a hint and a lesson to all those who are seeking truth, not from curiosity or passion for experiments—terms which in this case would be improper—but simply because they cannot help it, since it has become their very life?

The peak of Arunachala points the way upwards, a way always the same and unchangeable throughout the ages. It speaks to us in the language of silence as Maharshi does. What is the link and relation between them? I only know that the mysterious—to use the worldly term—atmosphere of the sacred hill has made me experience the reality of spiritual influences, which always come to us when the time is ripe. Without definite experience of this kind we could not have any certainty on the path. Theories will fall into dust at the first trial, or they will simply be forgotten as unable to help in our struggle. They have the same source as the mind which is, according to the Sage of Arunachala, 'a mere conglomeration of thoughts'.

On what would I concentrate or where would I find my life had I not had beforehand experiences transcending the limits of the individual, earthly consciousness? For all I am able to feel or think through my physical body will have to be discarded together with it as their source. Yes, it is now perfectly clear.

But shall I be able to remember it all the time and not submit to external happenings, nor allow them to draw me away from the

Truth which I have once seen? Shall I be able not to deviate from the one straight line during the long file of equal days to come? An inner voice which I *must trust*, says: 'No, not yet'. That means I shall still be at the mercy of ups and downs, of flight and fall, of light and darkness. It is the fate of every student in the great school of life. Whoever has reached the state of an uninterrupted union with, or merging in truth is a master, a superman. He is one for ever with the Source of his inspiration, the mysterious Arunachala. At the feet of such a great one I now have the privilege to abide.

Nothing can happen without a purpose, or in vain. The light of Arunachala will show me further steps upwards, as it has already revealed the meaning of the most enigmatic of all truths: '*To live one must lose oneself*', that is our transient 'I'. As Maharshi points out:

'Here on earth there exists a rare remedy which helps those who have recognized the illusory character of their personality, to discard and even destroy it, without destroying themselves physically. Know it to be none other than this Great Arunachala'.

*   *   *

Now once more I see the massive body of the sacred hill, the moon is much nearer the horizon and the dark shadows are deepened by black clouds which have come from the sea, from the east. It must be late. No light is visible in the Ashram at the foot of the hill, and no steps nor sounds of voices are heard on the highroad which encircles Arunachala.

All is silence and peace.

The fresh eastern breeze is now blowing.

CHAPTER XXXI

God

The thoughts about God came to me after a long stay in the Ashram, at the end of my period of silence, called 'mouna'.

Western beliefs, imposed on us and assimilated from our childhood, such as the idea of an anthropomorphic Highest Being, were not so easily transformed into less naïve and deeper conceptions. Although some years before my coming to India the grosser forms of religious prejudices had already been discarded—I mean the formal not the spiritual side, present in every religion—yet their discarding proved quite insufficient in the atmosphere of Maharshi. Being near him one feels the presence of God as a matter of course—no arguments or proofs are necessary. It is extremely difficult to express in words what the mind can never grasp. The Sage continually repeats that God can be known only subjectively, never as something outside ourselves, but rather as our own *real life*, our own innermost core or being.

Happily at one of my meditations at the feet of the Saint, just before closing 'the gates of the mind' for the exclusion of all thoughts, I remembered the words of the Master:

'All religious and philosophical systems can lead men only to a certain point—always the same—to the emotional-mental conception of God. And what is most important, meriting the name of true Achievement, lies beyond it, in *realization*'.

We do not then think about the Highest Being as dwelling somewhere in heaven, or as the primary cause, or beginning of all things, the primal movement that creates the universe, or in any other clear, comforting mental conception, for none of these speculations bring us nearer to reality.

'We should experience God in a more realistic way, every day, every minute, every second. In other words we should feel *being*

I

in Him, as this is the Truth. *He is* the only Reality, the basic principle of everything we see and experience'.

From Maharshi's Sayings

The mind is unable to grasp this simple truth, that God is really in everything, and not in some 'chosen' forms only, in some peculiar physical, mental or emotional phenomena. That *He* dwells in Maharshi as well as in each one of these primitive Dravidian villagers who sit in the hall, whose thinking processes are quite childish compared with those of the Brahmin meditating nearby. That *He* is in the refreshing evening breeze and equally in the black mosquitoes which annoy me even in the temple hall. That all kinds of deep-sea monsters which ruthlessly devour each other, as well as the silent prayers of devotees sitting at the feet of the Sage, breathe the same *life* of the Most High, and that nothing, literally *no thing*, is 'outside' His consciousness. Hence all is as it should be; nothing can go against His will, or exist outside Him.

The unruffled peace of the Master, the never disturbed calm, have not these their source in an *experienced* knowledge of these facts? Yes, it must be so.

If it is true, then nothing in this world can be 'alien' to me, nor can I ever be 'lonely'. And usually it is this loneliness that terrifies people so greatly. I now find the explanation of the overwhelming bliss one feels in meditation, as well as a sense of immortality which penetrates into one's consciousness slowly, gradually, imperceptibly, yet with unshakable certitude. If I am *All* that is, how can I lose life which is in truth the core of everything?

All these thoughts, however speedily they flash through my consciousness, begin to be tiring. Is it always necessary to keep on proving to oneself and repeating indefinitely that two and two make four, when one is now at His very feet? I want to *live* fully, in the real sense of the word. And Maharshi says strictly and emphatically: 'True Life begins when all *Forms* are discarded, all thoughts transcended, and only the Real *Self* remains'.

But this *Self* has nothing in common with that which is called 'I' on the physical plane of being. This illusory 'I' sits, abandoned there at the column, its life having taken for the time being the vegetative mode when the great breath is *turned inwards* to the Self. And the Real Self is something infinitely greater, more subtle and free. It is in *All and all is in Him*—That is God.

When we understand this, we begin to see that in truth every being seeks, albeit unconsciously, its source which is the Highest. The eyes are then open to the meaning of many inspired words of great poets and mystics, and see their hidden longing to be always turned inwards, to the same *one source*.

O world, why in the midst of your ghastly, unreal existence, are you unable to see the truth that there is not, and cannot be, any other goal?

Love and devotion for the Highest—the One—is then born spontaneously, with no questionings nor inquiries, but with full awareness that this is in the natural order of things, that everything *is* as it should be, that all His decrees are always just and right. If we are unable to perceive this, it is no fault of the *sun* who sheds His rays always and everywhere, but of the blind man, who does not see them. The capacity of seeing the sun is born in the heart not in the brain. This 'seeing' has nothing in common with the ordinary earthly perception like: 'I am here and He is there'. Such a mental concept is a definite obstacle to meditation, which can give us the first glimpse of the *sunbeams*. We should not try to pull down the *sun*—vain attempt—to our own level, but on the contrary we must step out of our small 'I' and go forward to meet the Light. This comparison, although clumsy and utterly inadequate, may reflect something of the attitude in which we have to start our battle for *life*.

All that can be said about the stages of our search for God is contained, in its fullness, in *silence*. Out of this silence one may draw endless pictures and definitions, but unavoidably they will all be imperfect, giving no adequate idea of the essence of the process. It would probably be wiser to plunge ourselves into silence, instead of listening to 'second-hand' experiences of those few who, in a greater or lesser degree, have 'learned' this art of silence. God speaks to us in silence, but we rarely allow the silence to come, or listen for Him to speak. For—we still do not know. In our ignorance we do not usually like silence, it bores us. We cannot imagine life without thought. But this illusory existence is not life at all; rather it is death, for death is the unavoidable end of all forms, particularly in the case of such an imperfect one as our little self—our 'ego', We close our eyes and do not want to see this obvious and somewhat terrible truth. In vain is this attitude which leads us nowhere! Just as a leaf torn from a tree can never return to it, so our transitory form will never be able to express our real Self.

A great teacher said clearly: 'No man can serve two masters . . . God and Mammon'.

In meditation one can perceive instances of God's intervention even in our daily lives; things which were unnoticed before become obvious. And our hearts are filled with immeasurable love, devotion and gratitude. Then we are nearing that state which Maharshi spoke of as 'a daily communion with God'. This is the goal and the summit.

But in our immediate future we shall probably gain only now and then some flashes of light, and not yet be able to abide permanently in Him. I fully realize that the Saint whom I am facing dwells uninterruptedly in the orb of light. This light is utterly different from any physical one we know, it is pouring even through closed eyelids.

'That' which was left by 'me' down there, at the temple column, has its eyes closed and certainly can see nothing. It is soundless and dumb like a corpse.

But there is the joyous and certain hope of resurrection.

I hear, as from a great distance, the Ashram gong.

CHAPTER XXXII

Some Remembrances

Today before noon Maharshi said he remembered me from the photograph of the 'Arunachala Group' in Brazil, sent to him in 1947 from Curitiba. He inquired about the little book published there in 1948, and whether or not I was the author of it. He asked the attendant to bring a copy from the Ashram library and inquired about its contents. I explained as well as I could, with the help of one of the Brahmin attendants. I told him that I was the author, and that I had myself typed the original which was then translated in Portuguese and published in Brazil. I went to my hut and brought a nicely bound copy with Maharshi's picture and that of the Brazilian 'Arunachala Group' dedicated to him. Then, to my great astonishment, Maharshi began to turn the pages—about a hundred—as carefully and slowly as if he were reading this unknown language. From time to time he directed his penetrating gaze upon me and then once again looked into the book. At last he put it on his knees and spoke to the attendant in Tamil. As soon as he finished, the Brahmin approached me and explained that it was the wish of 'Bhagavan' (it is the name given to Maharshi by his devotees and means 'the blessed one') to add notes giving the source of my quotations from Sankaracharya's *Viveka-Chudamani*, and listing those from the *Imitation of Christ* by Thomas a Kempis. Called by his gesture, I approached the Sage and took the book from his hands.

To fulfill Maharshi's wish I had to work several days in the Ashram library, where I had the kind co-operation of an American lady, a great devotee of Maharshi, who was only too glad to assist me in this fulfilment of his wish. I had to write it all in block letters to make it easier for the Saint to read, as my handwriting was not clear enough. At last, I was able to hand it over to the Master.

I was somewhat amused by the keen interest of the group of Westerners, especially one lady, a permanent resident of the Ashram, in the fact that Maharshi wanted to know all the details mentioned above. Yet they may have had a good reason for surprise: knowing the Saint's habitual indifference to all that happens down here, they certainly did not expect Him to pay such keen attention to anything.

I took the opportunity to tell Maharshi about the two groups in Paris and in Brazil, which take his teachings as the chief subject of their study, as well as the works of those who revere and admire him. He asked when and by whom they were started, what were the chief points of their studies, and so on. The smile which accompanied these questions was wonderful indeed. It seemed to encourage me, and this was indeed necessary, for how could one speak to him as one does to other people? Intuition definitely told me that not one word should be used which might be a platitude, that each and every one of them must be worthy of the listener. That was why in the beginning of each conversation one had to go through something like shyness which, however, disappeared as soon as one looked into his eyes.

I doubt whether many people have had an opportunity of seeing in anyone's eyes so much sympathy, wisdom and understanding, or such an incredible loving kindness as radiated from those of Maharshi when he spoke to us.

A few weeks before when I did not yet know how to address the Sage, following the example of others I wrote a few sentences and handed them to him after the morning meditation. They did not ask any question, but only requested something which I repeated later on the eve of my departure from India, when I took leave of the Saint. Those few words contained an epitome of all that I was and am still needing to be, to follow the path shown by the Master.

I became aware of this when I had proof of his fulfilling this my only prayer. I had made no other. The fact that it transcended the limits of this my life, and that its fulfillment was possible only by one who was himself beyond what we call life and death, was a kind of assurance to me that this time I had not erred.

It is well known that Maharshi does not perform 'miracles', that he sometimes even makes gentle fun (the Sage never 'condemns' anything) of the so-called 'occult powers' or 'Siddhis' of Yogis and other self-styled 'supermen', who use their psychic powers to exercise an immediate influence on their surroundings. But what else are we to call those changes which take place in his presence in the consciousness of pupils who most sincerely seek for truth? How are we to explain the strange, almost unbelievable changes in circumstances which often accompany the modifications of our inner state of consciousness; or those cases of immediate assistance when it seemed that nothing could help any more? Very little is spoken about it; hence we do not know much. Those who have experienced such help rarely talk of it, except to their nearest companions in the search for truth.

The lack of any mysterious atmosphere around Maharshi, his utter simplicity and naturalness, create the feeling that even if some extraordinary and unbelievable 'miracle' did happen here in the hall, or under the bamboo roof near the library, it would not provoke more curiosity than do the subtle designs of the incense smoke, slowly rising to the feet of the Saint and then upwards to the high ceiling of the hall.

The greatest miracle is Maharshi himself. I know that not all are able to feel nor even guess it. Such miracles can be known only by plunging into silence and into our own depths. Some can never do this although each and every one feels the beneficial influence of the Great Rishi.

* * *

This morning there was a celebration of some Hindu Saint by garlanding and smearing with red powder the stone statues of the sacred cows, one of which stands in the Ashram grounds, near the fence on the side of the main road which encircles the hill.

Maharshi was sitting on a chair opposite the small shrine during the whole of the ceremony, surrounded by people chanting Mantras. As always he was the same—placid and quiet, with no sign of interest in the activity of those round him.

Some time afterwards I thought I had grasped the cause of this indifference. It is this: the Sage does not believe in the reality of this visible world, he knows it is only an illusion. Dwelling all the time on the plane which embraces the *whole* of existence, how could he be interested in tiny fragments of happenings which are as ephemeral as smoke?

It seemed to me that the most logical analysis of existence in time and space should make the above clear and obvious beyond a doubt. But I have also seen the difference between a mental concept and the *realization* of this truth. Of course it is good to have a right mental conception, for it may help us to avoid mistakes. It is comparatively easy to admit that there exists a point of view from which the farthest star and the tiniest ant at our feet are equally near to or equally far from our *consciousness*. But it is quite a different thing to *live* in this inner, yet all-embracing world.

If I had not been here, at the feet of one who has realized this state of consciousness, I should certainly have had no idea about such a possibility. But now hope has changed to certainty, because of the *presence* of the *living Example* who sheds his light all round.

The second part of the ceremony took place in the temple. Trays with sacred ashes and red powder were brought and we all put on our foreheads a token of that ancient symbol, whose spiritual meaning is now remembered only by the few.

CHAPTER XXXIII

Power in Us

'If the supreme truth remains unknown, the study of the scriptures is fruitless; even if the supreme truth is known the study of the scriptures is useless (the study of the letter alone is useless, the spirit must be sought out by intuition)'.

Viveka-Chudamani, by Sri Sankaracharya, Verse 61

These words of Sri Sankaracharya are of much value to those who may be somewhat discouraged through the reading of too many books and articles filled with technical terms of occult philosophy. If we try to learn with our mind-brain only, memory is burdened and we never gain that which we intuitively seek—true spiritual enlightenment from wisdom of the Self.

Those who are making real progress on the path know that the process is really reversed. When we reach the realm of reality or spirit, then all terms and systems become clear, but—never *before*. The life of Sri Maharshi is an excellent example.

As a youth, before his enlightenment he knew almost nothing about the Hindu scriptures. But afterwards, he understood everything easily and could give incomparable explanations based on his own spiritual wisdom. This is the only natural process. Perhaps a simile will explain this better: a person who knows only English would be unable to read another language such as French although it was the same alphabet. He must learn the language in order to use it correctly. So it is with the scriptures. They speak another tongue although they use the same words as ours.

This is not to say that reading is useless. As the inner wisdom grows in us we find great support in the scriptures for they describe what we are experiencing for ourselves. They provide authority and certainty for us on the path. The further the disciple goes, the less complicated becomes his mind, and then he is able to express in simple form and words, clear to all, what would previously have needed an elaborate discourse full of technical terms.

We can recognize the utter simplicity of the words of Christ, Buddha, Maharshi and all the great teachers of humanity. Compare them with those of modern philosophers in both the East and the West, and it is obvious where truth is and where lies only the theory of truth.

In order to pass from this dream-life of a separate ego-personality to the real existence as Self, we need that light of truth Itself, not just Its description, for that cannot help us.

Sri Maharshi, in giving us a formula of life in the modern form of Vichara, was putting into effect the old truth that even one maxim of a true Master, if put into practice, is sufficient to lead the aspirant to the blissful end—attainment.

An omnipotent but unknown power lies latent in every one of us. Sri Maharshi spoke about it many times, especially in his *Instructions to F. H. Humphreys* in his early years. This power must be uncovered, for without it—nothing can be gained. It is by no means uniform in its manifestations and it appears to the disciple (but *not* to the Master!) as having different aspects—Bhakti, Jnana, and so on. Some of us know that there is nothing to be compared with the grace of the presence of the Master to make this universal power available to us. And the indirect help of his grace has been experienced by many who strive to know the ultimate truth, to enter the inner world of their beloved Guru.

This power enables man to subdue his relentless mind, which is the first cause of his troubles, outer and inner alike. It gives him at last that wonderful inner certainty from which arise silence and peace. They who awaken this power within themselves know that it brings about the ultimate union, and through that, immortality. The best form of help for a seeker, is one by which he is not harassed with a great many teachings, dogmas and definitions, all of which come from outside. There is a better method, used only by the Master, and that is by speech, look, or silence (and in very rare cases, by touch) putting the aspirant in such a position that he himself may find the solution to his problems. Then such a solution will be of his own living wisdom. This is all that matters in the school of human life.

In the foreword to the book *Maha Yoga* by 'Who', the author advises us to forget our relative science—which in reality is ignorance—before we can enter on the path. Obviously it is a condition and we should know why and how.

But it is not easy. Most people have great difficulty in getting rid of previous theories and former knowledge. But some are successful. And here a question arises: 'Why should we collect rubbish if it is to be discarded later?' Sapienti sat, as the Romans used to say.

Many sincere seekers are worried because they cannot acquire all the knowledge about religions, yogas, different occult systems, and so on. To these the advice of *Maha Yoga* is that the process of unlearning relative knowledge is not like forgetting it, but storing and locking it up in the mind-brain, and putting the key in the pocket. Then when you need to, you can unlock the store and use what you want. But do not spend your life indefinitely inspecting your temporary possessions!

*   *   *

It is better not to name this universal power here. It will be found in due course, and there is no possibility of a mistake. It is unique, alone and close to each man's heart. It can be relied on to accomplish any task. You will find it by your own effort. There is nothing apart from *it*, for *it* is the very core of your being, the ultimate—the ever-present goal, the only true and eternal friend.

The Great Rishi once said to a Westerner: 'When a man for the first time recognizes his true Self, then from the depths of his being arises something . . . And *it* then takes possession of him. *It* is on the other side of the mind. *It* is infinite, divine and eternal . . .

'The phenomena we see, are curious and surprising—but the most marvellous of all we do not realize, namely that *one* and only *one* illimitable force is responsible for all the phenomena we see, and for the *act* of seeing them.

'Do not fix your attention on all these changing things of life, death and phenomena. Do not even think of the actual act of seeing or perceiving, but only of that which sees all these things, *that which is responsible* for it all . . . Try to keep the mind unshakenly fixed on *that* which Sees. It is inside yourself . . .

'These things which we see and sense, are only the split-up colours of the *one illimitable spirit*.

'A Master in meditation, though the eyes and ears be open, fixes his attention so firmly on *that which sees* that he neither sees nor hears, nor has any physical consciousness at all—nor mental either, but only spiritual'.

These words of Sri Maharshi are the best explanation of the Power in us. There is nothing to add.

CHAPTER XXXIV

Correspondence

In letters received from America and elsewhere I often find the following questions:

'Which of the instructions on meditation given by ancient Indian philosophers are regarded in the Ashram as having most in common with Maharshi's teachings?'

Or: 'What should be our attitude towards our own personality when we are trying to follow the path of self-knowledge?' And so on . . .

The answers which I found here at Maharshi's feet may be useful to other people for the solution of the same problems. For their sake, therefore, I give in this chapter some excerpts from my correspondence.

Maharshi highly appreciates Sri Sankaracharya's *'Viveka-Chudamani'* or *The Crest Jewel of Wisdom*. Many Hindus regard the Sage of Arunachala to be a reincarnation of the author of this treatise, which reaches the highest summit of occult philosophic conception. I have chosen from it a few verses for my daily meditation, and I quote them here.* The word 'Brahman' denotes the Highest Divinity and 'Parabrahman' the Absolute; 'Logos' corresponds to the 'Creator of the Universe' or 'Demiurgos'.

Verse 409

The wise man in Samadhi perceives in his heart That something which is eternal Knowledge, pure Bliss, incomparable, eternally free, actionless, as limitless as space, stainless, without distinction of subject and object, and which is all-pervading Brahman (in essence).

---

*Note: Translation by Mohini M. Chatterji, published in 'A Compendium of the Raja Yoja Philosophy, comprising the principal treatises of Shrimat Sankaracharya and other renowned authors' by Tookaram Tatya, (Bombay, 1888).

Verse 255

Realize that thou art 'That'—Brahman which is far beyond caste, worldly wisdom, family and clan, devoid of name, form, qualities and defects, beyond time, space and objects of consciousness.

Verse 256

Realize that thou art 'That'—Brahman which is supreme, beyond the range of all speech, but which may be known through the eye of pure wisdom. It is pure, absolute consciousness, the eternal substance.

Verse 257

Realize that thou art 'That'—Brahman which is untouched by the six human infirmities (hunger, thirst, greed, delusion, decay, and death)—it is realized in the heart of Yogis (in Samadhi), it cannot be perceived by the senses, it is imperceptible by intellect or mind.

Verse 258

Realize that thou art 'That'—Brahman on which rests the world, created through ignorance, It (Brahman) is self-sustained, It is different from (relative) truth, and from untruth, indivisible, beyond mental representation.

Verse 260

Realize that thou art 'That'—Brahman which is the cessation of all differentiation, which never changes its nature, and is as unmoved as a waveless ocean, eternally unconditioned and undivided.

Verse 261

Realize that thou art 'That'—Brahman which is the one only Reality, the cause of multiplicity, the cause that eliminates other causes, different from the law of cause and effect.

Verse 263

Realize that thou art 'That'—Brahman that Reality which manifests as many through the illusions of name, form, qualities, change, but is yet unchanged like gold (in the various forms of golden ornaments).

Verse 264

Realize that thou art 'That'—Brahman which alone shines, which is beyond the Logos, all pervading, uniform, truth, consciousness, bliss, having no end, indestructible.

What lofty peaks of spiritual conception, rising straight up into the realm of the infinite, where truth reigns supreme!

The student of Self-knowledge begins to understand that his personality is a focus or fulcrum, as it were, through which flows and shines the light of life that is God. But he himself is *not* this focus. He must take care to maintain it in perfect purity, to enable the maximum of light to shine through it. But this should be his only care and nothing more. Herein lies the mystery of the disappearance of the 'ego' as the result of Self-realization. It brings true freedom. When the focus has fulfilled its task it is discarded with neither pain nor regret. But this happens only when it has become a lived reality and not a theory. And that is the highest initiation.

In any event one thing is true: only a balanced and one-pointed mind leads to the realm of truth—to Samadhi. Interruptions in the state of Samadhi prove that the mind is not completely subdued; it comes back to activity and evades the still imperfect control.

What kind of attitude is proper in the presence of the Master?

Nothing is more helpful in the presence of a great being than stillness of mind. It opens the door of our heart and enables the Master to come in. The proximity of Maharshi makes this effort of stilling the mind infinitely easier than it would be elsewhere. Often, even when people pray according to their own faiths, the result can ultimately be the same. In the presence of Bhagavan Maharshi we are able to find intuitively by ourselves the proper attitude.

The Self and the visible world.

An extensive explanation has been given by Maharshi himself in his 'Gospel'. So there is nothing to add. Nevertheless, as you want some 'physical' analogy a rough one may be quoted:

Suppose a pianist is playing in gloves, you will see only the leather out of which they are made, having the shape of the hand. The fingers as they *really* are cannot be seen. An ignorant person can believe that the leather of the gloves forms an integral part of the hands of the artist. In a similar way people who know nothing about the Self are unable to see anything beyond the physical side of things.

But he who sees reality knows that there is a hand which strikes the keys and plays the music, that the glove without this living hand inside is nothing more than a mere lifeless shell or vehicle.

The inadequacy of this analogy is that in truth you can never see the hand in the glove, for then you would be 'the hand itself'.

'*To see God is to be God*'.—From *Maharshi's Gospel*.

Initiatory societies

You ask: 'What about the numerous initiatory societies existing in the modern world?' Let us not be misguided. If you want to give me a glass of water, you must have water to give. Unless leaders of such organizations are true Masters—perfect men—their teachings and books can be little better than the mental speculation of a layman. The teaching must be supported by the *lives* of the teachers and give us an unmistakable example of true realization. Your own Self will never accept anything less. And until now I have never seen a Master running an organization or a business. Think it over and the answer will come of itself.

Obstacles to the realization of the Self

'They are your wandering mind and perverted ways of life', says Maharshi in his *Gospel*. Egotism and the identification of yourself with the physical body are the roots of ignorance, they prevent you from entering the Path and realizing Vichara—Self-Inquiry—'Who Am I?'

'I am this Mr. X of a certain age, appearance, position in society, nationality, profession and so on. I am born and I must die'. All of these *must* go before you will find an answer to your 'Vichara'.

A Yogi said: 'The Self of the seeker who surrenders himself to the Truth is merging into the Great Infinite Self'.

That is the path.

Prayer

You say: 'I am a Christian and a believer. I am unable to meditate, I can only pray. What achievement is possible for me?'

Achievement is the same for all. But the ways to it can be seen differently. If you study the lives of the Saints of all faiths, you will find that they are all brothers in the love and realization of God. Let our prayers be unselfish, and remember always that the Lord knows better how to rule His universe than we do. Therefore, He does not need our suggestions in the matter. Try to make perfect that which is really yours—your own consciousness. That is our only aim. I will give a beautiful example of a mystic prayer from St. Francis of Assissi:

'Lord, make me an instrument of Thy peace; where there is hatred, let me sow love; where there is injury, let me sow pardon; where there is doubt, let me sow faith; where there is despair— hope; where there is darkness—Light; where there is sadness, let me sow joy'.

'O Divine Master, grant that I may not so much seek to be consoled as to console, to be understood as to understand, to be loved as to love; for it is in giving that we receive. It is in pardoning that we are pardoned. And it is in dying that we are born into *Eternal Life*'.

The grace of the Master

Maharshi has written in his *Gospel* that this grace is too subtle to be described. Certainly he knows this far better than we do. Therefore, all attempts to explain in words what words cannot express are useless. Maharshi is always referring to grace as working on its proper level of spiritual reality, and yet you insist on obtaining an answer in words, which means within limitations imposed by our minds. It can be taken for granted that 'the attention' paid by the Master to his disciple can be regarded as one of the characteristics of his relation to him. Therefore, let us be worthy of such attention.

Surrender

Surrender is the state of consciousness which is a condition of discipleship. When the disciple realizes that his 'ego'—personality —is only a small ripple on the surface of the infinite ocean of the Self—or 'Overself'—which is reality, he deliberately begins to turn his attention away from it and tries to merge in that 'all' which generally takes the form of the Master. That is why surrender to the Master is a necessary step towards the ultimate goal, for it means the realization of the true Self or God.

Love

I do not remember who described love as 'a universal power of mutual attraction (gravitation) acting everywhere between atoms —which represent the material veil of the universe—as well as between other different manifestations of consciousness'.

Perhaps there is some truth in these words, although when expressed in the world of relativity, they must necessarily be imperfect. But practically speaking, love is the only power that can support our effort to step out of conditioned relativity into reality. On the hard path to realization any mental conception of the true goal, however lofty and sublime it may appear to us, will prove insufficient, because it is bound to disappear, together with the dissolution of our individual minds when they return to the one ocean of life. In other words the man who is struggling on the path to realization knows how much he needs this motive-power of love to overcome all obstacles. In occult literature there are many proofs of this. It is good to remember the well-known words of St. Paul:

'And though I have the gift of prophecy, and understand all mysteries, and all knowledge; and though I have all faith, so that I could remove mountains, and have not *charity*, I am nothing'.

Only the reflection of Truth itself can help us. Love *is* this reflection. And the highest form of love accessible to us is our love for the Master. The Master cannot come to an unloving disciple—if such a disciple could exist—just as light cannot penetrate into a room without windows. Nothing can help the pupil if he has no love. He must have a living example, and an ideal which is above all doubts and imperfections.

The Master

You say you know that without the Master there is no path, and you ask me, who am now at the feet of Bhagavan Maharshi: 'How is this truth realized in his presence?' If you could come here and sit under the bamboo roof extending above Maharshi's couch no answer would be necessary. You have some photographs of Arunachala hill, but you will admit that it is not the same as if you could climb, or see for yourself, the Hill of Grace. The same is true of the presence of Maharshi. You will find in this diary some of my personal experiences of it.

Control of the mind

'Submit to me and I will strike down the Mind'.

From *Maharshi's Sayings*

These words of the Sage may be the best answer to your question. Anyhow, every time that I am absorbed in the thought of Bhagavan no other unwanted idea can creep into my mind. Hence no futile or evil thought has any access to my consciousness. The habit of harbouring and feeding restless thoughts is now being replaced by the unruffled calm and peace of the mind. But this is not sufficient for the Vichara, or Path of Inquiry, '*Who Am I?*' as taught by Maharshi. A complete silence or stillness of the mind is essential. I have found considerable help in long and cool meditations on the origin of the thinking process, and curiosity as the source of thoughts.

Then I recognized that 'no thought can help me or change my so-called future', and so on. We are simply duped by our mind which suggests the idea of the 'necessity of thinking'. This subtle lie is hard to eradicate and hard to explain, because we are practically unable to stop our thinking process at will unless we are to a certain extent in that state of consciousness which extends beyond the mind. This higher consciousness—the mysterious 'Samadhi'— is the very aim of all seekers. As Maharshi said:

'Samadhi alone can reveal the Truth'.

From *Maharshi's Gospel*

Samadhi

There are a few descriptions of the transcendent state of spiritual ecstasy called Samadhi. There are also several kinds of Samadhi. Maharshi says briefly and clearly: 'In Samadhi there is the feeling of "I-I" or "I am" and no thoughts'.

But no real description of this state of real being can assist us in its attainment. When Samadhi comes, people are generally astonished at how false had been their mental ideas about it.

* * *

These are some excerpts from letters I wrote from the Ashram in answer to my friends in other parts of the world interested in true spiritual endeavour, but unable to go to India and see Maharshi. In his atmosphere of light and peace I feel there is really only one great heart, of which the Sage of Arunachala so often speaks. Therefore my distant—in space—correspondents are in reality nearer to me now, than they were when I was in their immediate physical presence.

CHAPTER XXXV

I and You

There is a considerable difference in my states of consciousness at different times. Often in meditation I experience the ecstasy of absolute union. But this is lost when I return to conventional life. It worries me somewhat; but the cause lies in the doubts generated by the mind. Therefore I strive to bring the light from the Inner Self to bear on it, and build a solid foundation in accordance with those spiritual experiences which are the only real consciousness. Then comes the necessity to translate them, if possible, into the language of the mind. Since the mind itself is only a reflection in the realm of conditioned life, symbols and comparisons are appropriate to the purpose, and in fact are the only means of conveying some ideas.

In the light of my previous experiences during meditation I offer this simile: individual personalities can be compared to the leaves of a tree. They are numerous, but their common life is that of the tree. It is the source of their existence. The leaves grow, fade and finally die. But the tree is unaffected by the fate of its individual offspring. It has no favourite leaves; it knows their temporary role, but do the leaves know the destiny of their mother, the tree, whose lifespan transcends by far that of each one of them?

Their life is possible only so long as they are unseparated from the mother trunk. All of them strive after more sun and air, albeit unconsciously. They cannot of their own will leave the tree before they are ripe and this ripeness means dissolution of their form.

From the point of view of the leaf, its life is limited, its possibilities circumscribed, and any efforts to avoid the common fate are in vain. Could it but realize that the continuing life of the tree is the only thing that matters; that to carry out its function faithfully is the only way in which it can increase the life of the tree on which its own well-being depends, as well as that of all its fellows.

It is tragic how we believe that our separateness is real, that what we have is our own, and so remain untouched by the needs of others. Like the leaves of the tree, at the appointed time, our outer shell must fade and die, and the ever-living Self be drawn back into its source. Real life is truly only in *That*.

Now my mind becomes quieter, for it has been told the truth in its own language. The realized unity is the Life of the spirit in the realm of the eternal. The illusion of separation is death.

The lack of egotism in great beings is not based on sentimentality or theory. They *know* their source. When Christ prayed for His enemies and when Maharshi, beaten by thieves, turned his other side to their blows—They knew the law. There was no hypocrisy in Their acts. They were aware that the same life flows through Their tormentors as through Themselves. The only difference lay in the fact that Christ and Maharshi recognized their oneness while the murderers and thieves did not.

In the simile of the tree and the leaves, the only difference is in the temporary form and colour of the leaves. So even the understanding of the law of Life compels us to transfer our consciousness to the spiritual realm, though but for a moment. If we have grasped with the mind the unity of the spirit, we have lived for a moment in the sphere of the spirit.

Sometimes we are able to grasp and realize the mystical meaning of the teachings of the Master, but the Self-oblivious personality forgets these important moments too easily.

'The Way is long. I am far from Home'.

CHAPTER XXXVI

Requiem

I usually dedicate one night in the week to meditation as a kind of continuation of our evening meditations in the presence of Maharshi. I do not write them down, for they are all similar and difficult to put into words. I can only say that they are an attempt to lift up my consciousness to the sphere where life alone reigns, with no forms and no veils. In the preliminary stage there is always a kind of struggle with all that prevents me from stepping out from the realm of thought; after that, like a film on a screen, appear the pictures of my past, and finally—usually about dawn— comes a moment of peace.

One July night however, I shall never forget, and its essence is expressed by the title of this chapter, for the period of my earthly life was buried definitely for ever. This life which until then, had usually claimed my attention and retrospective examination, quietly disappeared, swallowed up by that ocean of the unreal to which it has always belonged.

I did not then realize that only the present is existent, and that constantly returning to the past is equivalent to temporary suicide.

First I remembered a passage from a book based on the Hebrew Kabbalah, which many years ago had fascinated me with its mystery, but to the real meaning of which I could never find the key.

' . . . And the pupil entered the shrine of his heart. An altar was there and on it two lights were burning.

'He understood that these were the lights of his own life. They were himself. The flame of the nearer one was many-hued, pulsating with a richness of colour, and emanating a slight smoke. He recognized it to be his thoughts and emotions by the very familiar rhythm of their vibrations.

'The second and farther light was colourless, but its rays were pervading everything and penetrating through the changing hues of the first one. Immovable in its pristine purity it was quietly burning, breathing a peace as great as eternity itself.

'Then a Rabbi dressed in white appeared, took both the lights in his hands and changed their places. "From this moment you will look through the light of eternity on that of the fleeting life, instead of looking, as you have done till now, through the ephemeral light, which made the perception of the eternal difficult".'

*　　*　　*

'Who Am I? Who Am I? Who Am I?'—I plunged as usual into this meditative inquiry, and suddenly I saw my whole life, from its very beginning, hidden in the recesses of my memory, unroll before my eyes as if on a film. Looking at it, I once more went through the same experiences in a condensed and extremely rapid way. I sensed that I had the power to destroy this illusory picture by an effort of will, for it was weighing on me unpleasantly. And I also knew that it was not advisable to allow those illusory, nonexistent things to enter into my consciousness. But this time a voice which I had to obey told me to look at the 'film'.

Before me unrolled the years of my youth, with their foolishness and dash, instinctive life with its almost animal selfishness; circumstances and people, who at the time had played a great role in my life, loves and hates, noble and mean impulses, a search for something which was always evading my touch and which, when it seemed near, was continually slipping out of my hands. Moments of despair which seemed fathomless, hopeless, and without issue; moments of tremendous, one could almost say boundless 'happiness'—all passed before my eyes. The physical figure, so well known, gradually changing with the flow of years, now condensed, passed before me with all its hopes and dreams and endeavours of which nothing now remained. The years of the first and second world wars, the interval of peace, my plunge into occult studies where highest achievements seemed to lie, cosmoconceptions gradually changing through contact with new theories and their authors.

I felt it all like a dense dark cloud descending upon my consciousness; I was seeking an issue; intuitively I felt that it must exist, that now, when I stood on the threshold of a new life, I could not return to those ghosts.

Concentrating all my powers in one effort of will I stopped the weird chain, and in one moment when the 'film' stood like a dead thing, I understood beyond the shadow of a doubt: all this—it was not *me*. This actor and the surrounding scenery and decorations were not, and could never have been Myself. I was not now concerned with the shallow experiences, foolish endeavours, aimless thoughts, changing feelings and moods, and all the rest that some time ago had seemed to constitute 'Me'. I could now criticize and help others to criticize this 'person', a thing which I had formerly vividly resented, but which I could now do freely. Why? It was not the mind that was responsible, but this peace, this merging into the translucent, immaterial Self, and perhaps—the pushing to the second plane of the 'first light', according to the Hebrew tale.

All my attempts to find reasons have now no meaning. I have lost all interest in these definitions and explanations. Life has proved to be quite different from current conceptions about it—yes, it has proved rather to be the denial of them.

'Whosoever shall seek to save his life shall lose it; and whosoever shall lose his life shall preserve it'.

These words of the Great Teacher, once so mysterious and incomprehensible, are now a bright and radiant truth, in spite of the fact that they were pronounced two thousand years ago. It is little wonder that one also remembers:

'Heaven and earth shall pass away: but my words shall not pass away'.

In the silence which followed this more 'active' part of my meditation, hours passed unnoticed. I began to hear sounds from without, the voices of some wild animals approaching the Ashram's compound during the night, when no human being was about. I opened my eyes to look out of the window, and through the iron bars and wire net, I saw a big hairy head; it was a monkey, who, awakened by the approaching dawn, had come here from the Hill in search of mango peelings.

*   *   *

The day is beginning, a new day in this peaceful corner of the world, at the foot of the sacred Hill of Arunachala, chosen by the Master as his life's abode. It is true that here nature itself seems to assist human beings in their endeavours, for in spite of being in the tropics, it does not hinder one by causing excessive physical exhaustion. Is it the influence of the dry climate, or of the mysterious magnetism about which one hears so much? I do not know. I can only say that from the spiritual side, I have never met in my life with such suitable and helpful surroundings, and such a wonderful atmosphere radiating everywhere.

I begin to feel almost instinctively that the time is nearing when I shall not be able to benefit any more from this immediate and marvellous influence. Hence I am trying to get 'rooted' as deeply as possible in this spiritual soil, to take it with me for my further wanderings throughout the world.

I listen carefully to the melodies of the evening songs of meditation, linking them up with my present inner experiences. It may help me afterwards when, surrounded by an utterly different atmosphere, I try to live the same kind of life as now—at the feet of Maharshi. Intuition says that it is advisable to find some points of support which will prove useful, when in the very midst of the haste and noise of the Western world, I shall have to withdraw from it and return to the kingdom of silence.

But is not the best of all means already at my disposal? And Maharshi, whose very remembrance brings peace—can I ever forget the expression of his eyes during meditations in the temple?

Now when I write these lines in my cell during the hottest hours of the day, when all life seems to stand still, a mere word about Maharshi suffices to evoke his figure before my eyes, and all thoughts stop.

With this my writing must also stop.

CHAPTER XXXVII

The Last Days

I have just received a letter from Madras, informing me that my passage has been booked on a steamer sailing in a fortnight from Colombo. It means that in a few days I shall have to leave the Ashram and Maharshi. It means that the ecstatic evenings at the Master's feet which have transformed my whole being, showing vistas of a new and eternal life, have now to end.

Then what? Will there be a return to the old life? The mind does not give any answer—its silence is a trap. I know that it would be only too glad to resume its old habits of reasonings, doubts and looking for by-paths. But times have changed. Its life is no more *My* life, because my consciousness is now able to function without its medium and even in spite of it. It is not in the mind that I now concentrate my hope and trust. I remember well Maharshi's words:

'The mind has its role in the development of men, but this role is limited and can lead only to a certain level. Beyond it a new one begins'.

I see that the strongest weapon of the mind—curiosity and the passion for investigating transient things—does not find in me such a ready supporter as before. It now meets with criticism, born of a firm conviction that such a search leads nowhere, that it is just a vicious circle. This reflection suffices to re-establish peace.

O yes, I know that nothing can push me back into the former bypaths, whether I remain in the Ashram for the rest of my life, or leave it to wander through the world.

This awareness brings an incredible, overwhelming wave of joy, a stream of bliss beyond all words. It somewhat resembles the feeling of an all-embracing life which can never be extinguished.

I had not noticed how and when I got rid of the thought of and belief in the existence of death, not through reasoning, but through immediate experience. I only now seem to remember that in my subconsciousness there were definite and repeated attempts to imagine myself facing death, forsaking my personality, and observing what then remained of myself. These almost unconscious exercises have proved that when I discard the instinctive attachment to the form and conditions of earthly life, when I am fully aware that the thing which has 'my name and appearance' in this conditioned world is only a dream, then still 'something' remains, independent and *self-sufficient*.

The readiness to leave 'everything' at any moment *is the gate which opens the way to the infinite*.

I had not noticed that in almost all circumstances, in happy as well as in painful happenings and experiences, in the background of my mind there is now always the hidden thought: 'All this has no real meaning'.

In what mysterious way the radiant vibrations of the consciousness of the Saint had been penetrating into the darkest corners of my mind, so limited, narrow and full of shadows, I did not know, nor did I see any reason to investigate. I understood well, not by the mind, but with all my heart, the joyous words of the great poet and mystic of India—Kabir, who, to the questions of his pupils: 'How do you *know* the mysteries of spiritual life?' and 'What can be known about the aim and destiny of human life?' answered in ecstatic rapture:

'Truth exists whether we know It or not, just like the Sun which always shines, whether a blind man sees it or not. It is not important whether I 'know' about the facts you ask, for—*He knows, HE KNOWS*'.

I remembered again from the biography of Maharshi that the life of Kabir had attracted his attention when he was a schoolboy of only fourteen, before he had met with any book about the higher spiritual life.

My pain, felt some time ago at the very thought of separation from the Master has now disappeared. Some of his words come to me in a strange way, like living answers, not from without as if from another man, but from within, from the depths of my own being. Just now I used a wrong expression, for can one say there are *other men*? Immediately a correction came and I grasped it and understood. How can I express my infinite gratitude for the immensity of kindness and assistance I am given? And once more the Master says without word or voice: 'Why have you this thought? Do earthly parents expect gratitude from their infant children for all their love and protection?'

The world does not know those occult ties between the sparks of consciousness which on the physical plane take human forms. The world may even laugh at things which are beyond its comprehension, not being contained in the sphere of three dimensions where weights and measures exist. Some years ago my reaction would have been an inner revolt and criticism. Today it is silence.

This silence tells me that in every fellow-man down here, the Master dwells, and that I should see Him in everyone's eyes. Where are all the 'differences' when one abides in the land of reality? Who has ever seen a shadow there?

*　　　*　　　*

During the last few days we were not allowed to meditate as usual for hours in the hall in the presence of Maharshi, for he was very weak after some new treatment. We could only enter through one door, salute the Saint, and go out through another one. This was chiefly done by visitors who came for a brief period and by the Hindu inmates of the Ashram.

One afternoon when only a young Brahmin, one of the two permanent attendants, was present, I also came into see Maharshi, at least for a moment. I felt a strange urge to obtain his approval, as it were, of all my efforts and of the modifications taking place in my consciousness under his influence. Intuition told me that I could not possibly put my trust—this rarest jewel—into better hands.

In our ordinary lives, how rare are people who can boast of having even one friend in the world worthy of their unconditioned, absolute confidence, which in practice means the possibility of uniting their consciousness with that of another. We generally like to show 'our best side' to others. We try to hide our disharmonies, fearing that the person whose friendship we seek will turn away from us. We have to watch over our words and gestures to avoid any possible discord. All this is neither natural nor sincere. Hypocrisy, although in a subtle form, hides its head behind such actions. But nothing of this kind can exist with Maharshi, we are certain that he knows and understands everything in us, that he never judges and that his attitude towards us can never be changed in spite of all our sins and imperfections, so clearly seen by him. And that is just the secret of his magic influence, of his wonderful way of helping us most efficiently to rid ourselves of all our defects and weaknesses. But I also know that there are certain conditions which make this inner change possible; not to adhere to them is a definite hindrance to our spiritual progress. Even the best camera cannot give a good picture unless the shutter opens properly, and if the shutter of our consciousness remains closed in the presence of the Master, how can we hope to receive the Light radiated by him?

In this I see the explanation of the fact that out of thousands of people who visited the Ashram of the Sage of Arunachala, very few were able to take full advantage of his light. Just now, in his presence, I see it clearly, but I may forget it when I have to return to worldly life and plunge into far less propitious circumstances. I am therefore anxious to write down my impressions now. Often people are unable to get rid of old prejudices, theories or accepted beliefs, and when they see Maharshi they try to give him the name of a 'Yogi', a 'Saint', a 'Mahatma', thus looking at him through their own inner coloured glasses, and labelling him by some well-known term to suit their own ideas which are the outcome of their spiritual ignorance.

Their reasoning runs more or less as follows: 'Yes, he is undoubtedly a Saint, yet there have been greater ones in the world—Buddha, Christ. They have certainly been quite different. We have Their teachings, and nobody can deny Their greatness'.

Others say: 'In the far-off Himalayas there are Yogis who are miracle workers, they have been living for hundreds of years and controlling the forces of Nature; are they not greater, or at least equal to Maharshi?' And so, instead of taking advantage of the living Presence, they dream about other Masters.

To these people I would like to say: 'Was it not about such as you that Christ said:'

'Having eyes, see ye not? And having ears, hear ye not?'

Not knowing anything about other great teachers save second-hand information learned from books about Them written by Their pupils or by later historians; not having themselves seen those personages during Their earthly wanderings, such people compare Them with a living presence, whose mission is to give us the eternal truth in a form most suitable for our times. Finding themselves face to face with the dignified and venerable presence of Maharshi, unable to feel his spiritual magnitude and glory, they still seem dissatisfied, perhaps longing to see some 'supernatural' phenomena, some dazzling light over the head of the Sage, or the instantaneous healing of their physical bodies, so immersed in sin and selfishness as they are. And if these wonders did happen, they might still disbelieve and look for hidden electric wires and lamps as agents of the 'miracles' performed, or attribute the healing to some new medicine recently taken.

If such people had lived two thousand years ago and had seen the Great Teacher whose authority they now quote being led through the streets to an apparently ignominious and terrible death, they would have shouted brutally with the crowd when He was on the Cross:

'*If thou be the Son of God, come down from the Cross*'.

It is about them that He said:

' . . . They seek a sign, and there shall no sign be given them'.

Are not all 'miracles' when performed among materialistic men utterly aimless? The reason why they take place so rarely and only under peculiar circumstances seems clear to me: Providence only allows them to happen if their results can bring a definite good.

CHAPTER XXXVIII

My New Conception of Life

One of the most difficult tasks facing me during my stay in the Ashram is the need to find a clear definition of my new conception of life as such. It seems to be a central point in me, round which everything revolves in the consciousness which is my 'Self'. This conception must be final and absolute, as no other one will be acceptable to my Self.

Out of hundreds of definitions which I have met, not one seemed to give a perfect synthesis. Those which are conditioned must be dropped as false. Those which use too abstract a terminology and are impossible to put into practice, seem to me mere mental acrobatics good for retired professors of theoretical philosophy, but not for a man who strives for spiritual attainment. Yet I know that there must exist one which will appeal to the depths of my being and which will provoke neither doubt nor criticism, for it will be in tune with my own inner experience.

All who have realized truth-life, speak of It with the greatest enthusiasm as the only goal, for the attainment of which everything should be sacrificed, since all else is an illusion. Yet their words seem like beautiful and charming sounds from an unknown instrument. In my search I had to discard all that is conditioned, limited by name and form. That which remains with no form nor veils must necessarily be life itself.

The process of inquiry—chiefly through meditation—has shown me that the more I discard the idea of the reality of the visible, the nearer I feel myself to be to my goal. What are the stages of this process in practice? Of course it is impossible to describe them in detail, but the general lines are simple enough. Beginning to meditate in utter peace and coolness on the relation of outward objects to my Self, I often seem to grasp the truth, that they do not mean anything to the 'Self'. In this moment dawns a kind of vision of

160

the possibility of *existence* independent of all conditions. This 'vision'—it is not a strict nor a quite suitable word—lasts for a shorter or longer time, depending on the degree of concentration achieved, but its results remain as memory of a thing lasting and certain beyond the shadow of a doubt. It finds expression in the thought: *'only consciousness is life'*. Consciousness unattached to anything, independent of everything, the bare assertion: 'I *Am*'.

But this 'I' is not the small self contained in the transient bodily form with its senses, which is in truth the antithesis of the real Self. This 'I'-consciousness is nearest to the term often used in modern philosophic literature—*'cosmic consciousness'*, or the *'cosmic self'*. This consciousness is also an *absolute bliss*.

L

CHAPTER XXXIX

'Seek ye first the Kingdom of God . . .'

'Seek ye first the Kingdom of God, and his righteousness; and all these things shall be added unto you'.

This sentence is the key to understanding the fate of our world. Providence will never forsake one who is really seeking for light. This, however, does not mean that spiritual search can bring worldly riches. But these 'riches' are not craved by the disciple of wisdom; he feels far happier and more free in possessing a very limited number of things, and desires that his means will be just enough to maintain his physical vehicle and its activity 'according to the great plan' as occultists say. These material possessions vary in quantity and quality according to the climate and the part of the globe where the disciple dwells. Maharshi could spend all his life with no other possessions than a small vessel for water (the traditional 'kamandulu') and a bamboo stick to help him climb the steep slopes of Arunachala. Clothes in this climate can be reduced to a loin-cloth, and the age-old simple ways of life, adopted by Indians as best suited to the tropics, reduce to a minimum the needs of a human being. But in other colder climates it is not so simple: our skin is not a sufficient protection against the changes of weather.

More garments are needed as well as suitable houses. These are necessary conditions of existence in colder countries, and this creates other needs and complications as regards the material side of life. Hence for us it is neither a sin nor a vanity to have somewhat more possessions than has the Sage of Arunachala. The problem lies not so much in the possessions themselves as in our attitude towards them. If we regard them as an unavoidable attribute of life on the physical plane, according to the exigencies of Nature, it is all right and they will not be an obstacle in our search for the Kingdom of Heaven.

But if we are continually running from one object of the senses to another and are full of craving, making the acquisition of possessions our chief goal and losing sight of the highest purposes of life, then we are not seeking truth but these 'other things'. In this case we obviously do not find either, for we have no permanent satisfaction from material possessions, and, as we desert our deeper being—called 'soul' in the Gospels—we prepare for ourselves further ages of suffering.

If we look round us, we must admit that in the present stage of evolution, the majority of people exist only for the satisfaction of a craving for worldly possessions, and do not see anything beyond. By the decrees of providence there are always less riches than selfish desires and appetites. Is it not to remind us of our true Goal? When the craving for possessions grows, there appear active attempts to take them from other—generally weaker—individuals or nations. And new waves of violence and evil are created, with their unavoidable result—*suffering*.

Suffering, so much hated and shunned by all human beings is, in fact, the only antidote neutralizing the poison of evil in ourselves. When, under mighty blows, glimpses of understanding of its cause dawn in our consciousness, our path, instead of descending lower and lower, begins to turn upward and mounts the ascending part of the arc of evolution. Then the 'search for truth' begins. When the time is ripe a definite turn upwards is made; we meet a Being who has completed this evolutionary course and has acquired the fullness of experience and wisdom. He is the perfect man, called by the Hindus the Guru, which literally means 'one who dispels darkness' and by the West—Master, Saint, Messenger of God. Everyone who is allowed by providence to meet and approach a Master is by that very fact partaking of His grace. It is a tremendous opportunity for growth and at the same time a great responsibility. According to the beliefs of my Hindu friends, which are based on the Vedas, there is no greater possible blunder in this life than to miss the opportunity thus sent to fulfil the intentions of the Most High.

In Maharshi's environment there are strange happenings too. Not all can stand the vibratory power of the invisible radiance of the presence of one who is pure spirit. There are cases of temporary or permanent loss of balance, of mental or emotional poise. There are extravagances, foolishnesses, and nonsensical actions performed with a belief in their reasonableness. But there are also cases where obvious inner disharmonies are healed in the presence of the Saint. Of course, those benefit most who can deeply understand the teachings of the Master and grasp their inner hidden meaning. Such a meaning undoubtedly exists, in spite of the utter simplicity and directness of Maharshi's words. It could not be otherwise, for his teachings belong to the realm of the Spirit, of Reality, and when re-veiled in words for our sake, in this very process their pristine purity must necessarily be modified by the limitations of mind, thought and word. The assimilation of Maharshi's teachings is a process similar to that of *remembering*. The Sage says that the real Self—(Truth—Spirit—God being different names for the same reality) is always and everywhere present. It is therefore also in our own consciousness, which ignorance covers with a veil of thoughts.

'All that is really necessary is the removal of the veils. Then the Light will shine by Itself and permeate all your being, then there is no need of seeking It somewhere else'.

From *Maharshi's Sayings*

The Kingdom of Heaven is within us, yet *we cannot remember it*. Were it not the greatest tragedy of Mankind, it could be regarded as a paradox or as a gigantic jest.

CHAPTER XL

What is Meditation?

Meditation can be properly performed only when the mind is cleansed of all thoughts. Almost every student of occultism knows of this condition, but—few can really achieve it.

Those who belong to different occult or mystical societies often believe that meditation consists in the effort of directing the mind into certain channels according to preconceived ideas. The results of such exercises—they cannot be called meditation—are generally poor, even though they may be practised over a period of years, and they do not lead to the effective purification of the mind from thought.

Usually, advanced members of such organizations are given methods and rules, which are often inefficient. There are two kinds which we can call artificial and natural means.

The first group is based on imagination or mental conceptions. Endless exercises are given, a few of the most important being:

(a) The imagining of the possession of a virtue lacking in the student. If he is of a sensual type, he must think of himself as chaste during the time appointed for the meditation.

(b) He can protect himself from invasion of thoughts from outside by the mental creation of an astral shell according to instruction.

(c) By the use of incantations or mantras he can reach the necessary concentration or acquiescence of mind, thus keeping to one idea for some considerable period of time.

In the second group (natural means) I would first mention prayer directed to what one believes to be the supreme being. If such prayer is utterly sincere, and if one is prepared to give enough time to regular practice, the result can be satisfactory and the mind cleared of everything but the object of meditation.

Then can come the '*vacuum*' in the thinking process, which is then filled with true light from its source—the Self-God.

If one is blessed on his way through life by meeting a spiritual Master, then everything becomes simple and effective. Many disciples in those precious times of spiritual contact visualize him as seen, in the physical body. Such an image, living and powerful, is a deadly weapon against the strategy of the restless mind. Nothing is more effective than this when combined with the Vichara; but in order to use Self-Inquiry properly, some steadiness of mind must first be attained.

Man's emotions must also be cleansed; for this purpose the vision of a living Master has no substitute. In a mysterious way the power of such a vision is also inherent in his (the Master's) pictures. Perhaps this is for the aid of those who were not able to see him in the physical body. Experience and practice show that almost as beneficial results can be brought about from the contemplation of such a picture. When at last the vacuum or void in consciousness is reached and firmly established, true meditation can be approached, but not earlier. Then the consciousness of the true Self will itself fill the vacuum. No more instruction is needed, for the true Self takes over the guidance and the goal is reached. In such meditation there are no visions or feelings. Maharshi often warned against ecstatic visions, pointing out that our goal is pure awareness and nothing else.

If this awareness is attained it inevitably leads us to Samadhi, and this is the true aim of meditation. Elsewhere in this book it is called 'the awakening from the dream-state called normal physical consciousness'.

There are signs which indicate that our meditation is really leading us to Samadhi, when we are free from all thought of the body and of the 'ego', and when thoughts and feelings are stilled. 'Good and evil' cease to exist—we see nothing, for there is nothing to see. Yet we are not in darkness, but merged in light being ourselves this light. We cannot see It for in this state there is no subject and no object. This can give but a veiled hint of the true state to one who has not experienced such meditation for himself, for this is the discovery of the true Self in man.

All that we recognize as objects—that is the outer world plus our visible body—is like a painting. The colours in it are the qualities of things. In these things are held all material forms, feelings, thoughts, good and evil, true and false, everything that we know as the universe.

They are like the separated colours of the white light or God-Self, broken up by the prism of the material universe, as the Maharshi told us. If you could imagine the same picture painted with only the basic white Light, unbroken by the bewitched prism —that would be Spirit, Self or God, the ultimate truth of being. That is why the Master said: 'There is nothing but the pure Being, which alone exists and our sole purpose in life is to realize It for ourselves'.

Right meditation leads to the discovery of this great mystery. All other means mentioned in different Yogas such as breath control, mind control, body postures, special foods and attitudes of the mind, and so on, are only intermediary steps on the path to the goal, taken by our material nature when we step onto the Direct Path to the summit. This attainment makes these intermediary steps unnecessary. When the train reaches a certain station, one does not go back to count the milestones already passed. Thus attunement with the Self produces of its own accord the right postures, breathing and imperviousness to influences from the outer world.

But this Direct Path is not suitable for everyone. The very fact that there are other Paths points to this.

Many Yogis whom I met, although fully conscious of the existence of this sublime path, continued to follow their own particular methods as proper for them in this life.

CHAPTER XLI

Techniques of Meditation

One of the initiations through which we pass while in the presence of the Maharshi, is true meditation which years of study of occult literature had assured me was the key to the awakening of supra-physical consciousness. During my allegiance to Theosophy I practised different forms of meditation in accordance with their literature. From what I have since found out, the knowledge given was for beginners.

Their aim was to direct the mind into certain deliberately chosen channels of thought. There were meditations on different themes such as Beauty, Love, Purity, Wisdom, Devotion, God, the Creator of the Universe and so on. The object was to keep these ideas in the mind as long as possible, and to imagine the working out of these virtues in the consciousness. Such 'meditations' can create certain currents of thought in the mind, conditioning it to a positive force which activates the thinking. Such exercises have a certain usefulness, for it is said 'a man is as he thinks'.

In other words the manner of a man's thinking creates his worthiness. If he associates himself with good and positive thoughts his nature will be improved; if with negative and evil currents—he will retrograde and fall. All this is true in the relative field, but is founded on the assumption that man's consciousness is derived from his thinking apparatus or mind.

Formerly it was impossible for me to conceive of anything beyond mind. Its ocean was shoreless, and from each island as I reached it, there appeared others still to be investigated. The goal could never be reached by this process. I know now that there is no limit to the mind's activity either for good or evil.

Man can elevate his mind, as do the Yogis, and perform 'miracles' as have many of the saints of all religions. The mind is a power, and when controlled and directed, its force and subtlety are apparently unlimited. But only apparently, for the power of the mind is based on the false notion that there is one who thinks, and an object of thought. This is the old lie of duality, and its end cannot be brought about by the ennoblement of the instrument.

The subject and object still exist. This conception hinders the realization of the unreality of the outer world. And to count this as real is an insurmountable obstacle on the path of realization of the true Self in man.

So long as a man's consciousness is unable to merge in the whole, there will always be the necessity for re-births and incarnations in matter. The bewitched circle is closed.

Strangely, from the first days of my stay at the Ashram, my old mental meditations were forgotten and I could not practise them in the presence of the Master. So it still is, and for me there will be no return to those old currents of thought. Every day there is a more and more urgent inner inclination to be still, to remain without thought, to merge in the silence. The inaudible inner voice tells me that there lies the truth.

Maharshi himself insisted on the necessity for meditation, but what did he mean by this term? He calls true meditation 'silence', 'being still', 'stillness'. So it was the same power which drew me then and now.

While one is immersed in water one cannot see anything above the water's surface. The world above is veiled from sight. To gain the wider horizon one has to rise out of the water, and only then will one realize how limited was one's former vision. So long as man is merged in the world of thought—the realm of mind—his consciousness will be bounded by its limitations.

Thought must always have an object, however sublime it may be, thus there must always be *two*, not *one*. Therefore thought and its processes is a blind alley.

The Master's power released me from all desire to follow this by-path. It was simply forgotten, as mentioned before. In a previous chapter of this diary it was said that I am not a believer in miracles. So I cannot put the help and activity of the Master into this category. But the fact remains, and that is all that matters. In this manner I came at last to the secret of true meditation. This state when I am aware of being apart from the thinking process can be called true meditation. This Awareness is the source of all Life, of that which is *my* life. It is the source of everything. From It alone I draw all that makes possible what I say on these pages. What I can express is tragically little.

When I first realized the impossibility of conveying anything more than fragments from this source, it seemed to me that the rest must be lost. After my first plunge into silence (see Chapter 'The Darshan Resumed'), I could not remember much about that experience and I simply said that the bridge was destroyed. Now it is different. Perhaps the mind-brain has learned to transmit something more of this higher realm of consciousness. It is immaterial what the reason is, the fact alone is important.

But how can one enter this state of supra-mental meditation? Analysing the process in myself, I find that *first*, must come the stopping of all thoughts. The Vichara ripens the mind so that interest in the thinking process vanishes, and the stilling of the mind, so difficult in the past, becomes easy.

Secondly, when the mind is still, there arises a strong urge to be united with the whole, but what this whole is, cannot yet be conceived and I feel that I could never attain it alone. The closest comparison is—melting and dissolving in That which alone *Is*. It is different to leaving the body or ego for there is no movement. One remains where one is, but is not what one was before. Everything that could be seen or felt before is now apart from me. No more can be told.

Thirdly, the state of unity with the whole brings an unshakable certainty that only this state is real and permanent. That it is that last refuge which one has always sought, and from which one can never more be lost. There is nothing beyond it, for—*it is all*.

The conception that we know as 'death' is obliterated, but this does not mean that we are in that state thought of as 'life after death'. The only fact one knows is, that this life will always go on.

In this state of being there are no such false distinctions of time as past, present, and future.

It is possible to force language to convey to the mind something of that which one brings back from such a meditation, but it is likely to be of no avail, and more likely to be misunderstood. And there is no certainty that others will come to this kind of silent meditation by the same way as oneself. So that any description can only suggest and even that may not be an appropriate path for another.

There is a mysterious experience which proves the power of the Vichara. The Master insisted that we should not use it as a Mantra, that is, as words only, but soak each question with the desire to know 'Who Am I?'. By using the Vichara in this way, after stilling the mind, the answer comes of itself, but without words or thought—you *know who you are*.

What follows—is inexpressible.

This is the great service which Maharshi performed for humanity—the welding of this infallible instrument of achievement, the inspired Vichara.

CHAPTER XLII

Departure

Two days more and I shall have to leave the Ashram. I have to pay several farewell visits to my friends. Some having learned that my departure is near come to see me in my cell for the last time.

I was feverish during these last evenings due to inoculations imposed on everybody who leaves India. In the tropics fever is felt more than in colder countries; but on the whole my body supported the beautiful climate of Tiruvannamalai quite well, and this fever brought on by an outside cause was the only indisposition during my entire stay in India.

I have first to go to Madras, to spend a few days in the magnificent headquarters of the Theosophical Society in Adyar, where I had already paid a short visit on my way to the Ashram. All kinds of formalities as regards transit visas will take several days. Then there will be a railway journey through South India to Ceylon, and finally—the Indian Ocean.

In my conversations with friends I expressed my belief—or rather premonition—that I should return to the Ashram before long; they also felt that we would meet again. But I did not speak to anyone about the second premonition, no, an inner certainty—that I should never more see the Master in his physical body.

I wrote this sentence almost unconsciously, and was myself terrified to read it. It meant that his place in the temple hall, in the dining-room, on the paths of the Ashram's Compound, would remain deserted and empty. How shall I bear this emptiness and darkness when the bright shining lamp disappears, the great lamp whose light truly dispels all 'darkness' in me? And my perfidious foe—the creator of thoughts—catches the chance of dealing me a blow: 'Oh, you have already buried the Master; while he is still alive, you are imagining how you will feel after his departure'.

This was too much for me, black lightning flashed in my brain.

It probably lasted for not more than a hundredth part of a second, but it was enough for Mr. X sitting by my side to seize my hand with alarm: 'What's the matter with you? What do you see?'— But it is over; the moment I asked the magic question 'Who Am I?' I recovered the balance, whose momentary loss might have been dangerous. In addition, I saw once more how illusory is the thing we call—*time*.

'A thousand years are like a day and one day is like a thousand years'.

The mystic sentence of the Bible sounds in my ears.

'Nothing special, dear doctor', I answered quietly. 'It is probably the result of that last cholera inoculation, such a formidable dose was injected by your nice Surgeon'.

'Although it is rather early and Bhagavan will not come for half an hour, yet I would gladly sit for a while in the hall; it is quiet now and probably quite empty', says my companion. We get up, my first steps are rather shaky. Have I to believe my own words about inoculation?

The time of my departure is fixed for the day after tomorrow, in the early morning. Tonight I must take leave of Maharshi and ask his permission to depart. This custom is a formality, but the deeper side of it is so much more important. These are the last hours in the immediate presence of the Master, the Friend, the Protector. They will never be repeated. What comfort shall I find, what Sun will warm the tiny germs born in the presence of the Great Rishi?

It is so silent in my room. The watchman has retired after having done his duty—bringing drinking water. The servant girl has also disappeared, using the few free hours before the meal for her own pleasure: she may carry bricks at a nearby building site. I bolt my door and sitting in a proper posture for meditation, I plunge with all my thoughts, worries and feelings into silence, the realm of the true Self. What a strange impression: the gradual disappearance of the outer world suffices to bring happiness. Even if this preliminary stage were not to be followed by higher grades, it would constitute in itself a kind of paradise. But it is only the outer court. Yet to reach this very outer court, thirty years of search were needed.

Some interference on the part of the mind is starting: 'so many things to be done', it says, 'several conversations, letters to be finished, a telegram to be sent to Madras and this thing and that'. But this time there is no struggle, nor effort to quieten it down. Who is interested in these petty things? Will not Someone greater take care of them when I neglect them? And thoughts disappear by themselves, as my interest in them ceases to exist.

I am now soaring in infinite 'space', strangely silent and empty, yet throbbing with intense life. No, I am mistaken in my attempt to put into words what words cannot contain, for in truth I do not feel any movement; rather 'this all' is flowing through me, and I am only a witness. In the next stage I utterly forget my personality (ego), its name, form, position; the consciousness of the separate 'I' is lost. The more light which can pass through the modest 'focus' of my consciousness, the less ties I feel linking me with the world. I am able, however, to stop in this flight and inquire—without thoughts—what is it that still binds me to *Maya* —the illusion of matter and form—and what more should I discard? But the overwhelming silence deprives these observations of any inquisitive outer character and changes them into a process of union with the *whole*.

This 'space' is peculiar, it is like the inner side of all possible physical spaces. So, by soaring in this 'inner' space one can be as near to the farthest star, as to the blood cell in the tiny vessels of our brain. To go through such transcendental experiences, one condition is necessary—it is the capacity to control and to stop at will the functions of the mind, that is, all thoughts.

The bright penetrating light shining 'here' shows me that I do not yet realize the nature of thoughts. I only know from the Master's teachings how we should treat them, and this from the practical side suffices to achieve the control.

I had just finished noticing these bits of thoughts, when a knock at the door brought me 'back' to my ordinary consciousness. It was the servant girl bringing in dried towels. She tries to explain to me in Tamil that it is noon and she must take the vessels and bring my meal. And with something of a smile she casts covetous glances towards my shelf where beautiful bananas are tempting her. Should I agree, she certainly would be happy to make a meal of this delicious fruit; but I try to convince her that fruit should be eaten only after a good meal of rice with ghee.

Yet even up to the time of my departure I never succeeded in convincing her.

CHAPTER XLIII

Farewell

I am returning from the temple hall, where people were passing before Maharshi's couch, as in a procession. I have not taken part in it. I am waiting for 6 p.m. when the flow of visitors stops. From six till seventy-thirty the Master is often alone. Hence it is the best time to approach and take leave of him.

The night is exceptionally hot with no breeze, not even a breath of the usual cooler eastern wind. The road is empty, and there is no one at the Ashram gate, only several motor cars stand in its large courtyard.

Twilight reigns in the temple hall. I stop for a moment at the door. Maharshi is sitting in his habitual posture, reclining on pillows and looking into space. One of the young attendants is sitting in a corner, almost invisible in its darkness. No one else is in the hall.

Maharshi now sees me and a slight smile appears. I approach him, but all the well-prepared words of farewell and the last requests disappear from my mind. It remains empty, there is not even a single thought.

I salute and stop quite near to him. He looks into my eyes. I plunge into the light of His. No words are now needed. I know that the Saint reads my heart. He has seen each word in my mind even before I put them together.

Deep down some sadness flutters in me. I see for the last time the one who is my Master and my Friend, whose like I shall never find again, were I to search all the worlds. Yet a subtle but irresistible wave of strength flows from Him. It carries away this cloud and penetrates through the whole of my being. Now my consciousness is pure and transparent, I feel it is thus that I wanted to stand before Him.

I see a kind of encouragement to express myself in words emanating from His beautiful face. Well, I say to myself, I shall try if it is necessary.

And I begin to tell Him slowly and clearly that I have to leave the Ashram and beg His permission, and after He nods in consent, I proceed to ask His blessing for my present, my future, and—for ever. His eyes seem even more luminous, the face, expressing a superhuman kindness, seems to become more serious. He gives me the blessing. I know He sees my next, still unexpressed entreaty. I do not hear any words, yet I feel He is asking me whether I am aware of the meaning of my own prayer. And, without moving my lips, I give Him my answer. Yet all is so natural, so simple, so real, that I would rather doubt my standing here than this mute conversation. A short silence follows.

O, I could stand like this, near him without end, for all eternity, with no other wish in my heart. Minutes seem to pass, though they may be only seconds.

The last request which I wanted to express is, according to the Master's teaching, a kind of concession to the visible, hence the unreal, world. It is for the pupil to have a visible, tangible sign of the Guru's grace, sanctified by ages of tradition. I had been told that Maharshi never gives it, and even in his biographies, I had read the answers given by him to such requests. It meant that he was careful and strict even with appearances.

But here, now, when I am standing before him with an open heart, feeling all that is taking place with joy and certainty, how could I be refused?

As soon as I begin my sentence somewhat shyly, his wonderful smile comes to encourage me.

I bow my head and feel the touch of his hand on my brow, the delicate touch of his fingers along my head. A subtle current of power and purity passes through my whole frame.

Like in a lightning flash I realize that the power of this moment will sustain me in all the years to come, and its light will for ever shine on my life.

We do not talk any more. I salute for the last time, he nods in

M

the Hindu way which denotes consent or approbation, and I withdraw slowly towards the door, looking at His face with all intensity, to engrave it for ever in the depths of my heart. I walk in a joyous peace back to my cell, through the dark paths of the garden. A few Ashram friends accompany me to my gate, in perfect silence, for Indians know how to behave in solemn moments.

The inner voice says: separation from the Master is no more possible. And so it has proved.

CHAPTER XLIV

Colombo

The Danushkodi Express is carrying me towards the South. My companions in the compartment are three Indian scientists, members of a scientific delegation from New Delhi. Two are going to London and one to Switzerland, the latter is a cultured physician, and author of several books in English. He inquires about the climate of Europe and asks if the cold is very severe. I inform him that November—he will arrive in Geneva in that month—will not be very pleasant to his taste, and add to myself, how happy I would be to feel that cool autumnal temperature of the Old Continent instead of this unbearable heat in our compartment. Two electric fans are working day and night, but it is not enough. The burning walls of the car give out heat on all sides. Fortunately my dress is as light as possible, shorts and thin open shirt.

I am looking through the window on a sad landscape, the sandy wastes of this last south-eastern part of the Indian Peninsula. People seem to be half-starved. Happily there are not so many beggars at the stations to approach the doors, for they are less hopeful of alms when they see only Indian faces in the compartment, and I am invisible from without, hidden in a corner under a fan.

At last we change for the boat which is to take us to the other shore—to Ceylon. After one more night in the train we reach Colombo. The Doctor takes leave and gives me a well-published pamphlet with a nice dedication. I find at the end of it a list of all the books written by him. My companions have to wait three days for their steamer. I have only two in which to visit Colombo. After our arrival I am going to look at the town and then at 4 p.m. find Mr. R., to whom I have an introduction from Madras. He is an elderly, handsome and cultured gentleman, an ardent devotee of Maharshi, and after a few words we became friends.

He takes me to his bungalow, about half an hour's journey by bus from the town. After my bath I put on Indian dress, most comfortable in this climate and meet my host on the spacious verandah, where a few of his friends, elderly gentlemen in spotless white, have gathered, and his son, a student of the Colombo University. We talk about our experiences in the Ashram, as all the guests have gone there several times, and naturally we talk about Maharshi himself. I am struck by the degree of devotion and veneration felt in their words about him. The West may envy this deep sense of reverence which makes Indians instinctively recognize spiritual greatness and saintliness wherever they meet it. How far we are from this quality! The West easily recognizes material power and fame, diplomas and certificates of learning and the quality of daring enterprise, but such a rare phenomenon as Maharshi would pass almost unnoticed. The West is seeking infallible solutions for its burning social and national problems, but strangely enough it does not see, or even avoids, those who have found the answer. And what is worse, the feverish hurry and materialism of the West has been communicated to some of the Eastern people, thus increasing their sufferings and the dangers around them.

Our conversation runs smoothly and harmoniously, no one wanting to convince the other or to impose his own opinions arbitrarily. We talk simply about our convictions and experiences, knowing that everyone may see a portion of truth and no one can possess It in its fullness. We are trying to find common points and principles and do not dwell on possible differences.

I think the basis of our understanding of each other is our common belief that the *One* who created this Universe for a purpose known only to Himself, also knows how to guide it in the best possible way. If one has such a firm belief, then all one's ambitions and desires to change the world drop away. We can see that these human ambitions in the past as well as in the present history of Mankind do not give satisfactory results. We all agree that the words of those who have seen Causes, in uniting their consciousness with that of the Highest, have more weight and value than those people who move among the shadows of the results, cast by causes to them invisible and unknown.

We are linked by our common reverence and love for Maharshi. All of us see in him the Master who enables us, in proportion to our spiritual capacity to see glimpses of Truth.

We speak of him, each one telling of his own experiences. We stop from time to time to feel more vividly the subtle spiritual current when the Master appears before our inner eyes. We understand each other so well in these moments; as if we had been friends for ages. No one interrupts the Silence, no one is bored by it. Alas, I shall never again be able to boast of our Western art of conversation.

Our host leaves us for a moment and we smell the subtle aroma of incense; when he returns he invites us with a grave and kindly gesture, in silence, to his little private shrine. A small altar with pictures of Indian Saints stands near the wall, with symbolic figures of deities beside it. A few mantras engraved in golden letters are hanging on the walls and complete the setting of this simple little shrine. A light is burning and incense sticks are before the altar. There is no other furniture save a few mats on the floor.

We sit in one row with crossed legs. I am in the middle with my host, and on his right his wife and son, who at his bidding recites a few verses from the Vedas. The incense smoke rises in thin spirals into the silent air. I think: 'Let our meditation—it may also be called "prayer"—rise like this smoke into those regions where sadness and darkness are unknown'. We plunge into Silence.

I do not doubt that my companions are in the same mood. It is the marvellous characteristic of the psychic atmosphere of some Eastern countries that thoughts and especially inner moods, are communicated more easily there than in other parts of our globe.

I see that my neighbours close their eyes for meditation. I do the same, although I have noticed of late, that when the concentration is thorough and the attention turned completely within, even open eyes see nothing.

After some time a kind of urge from without informs me that it is time to finish the meditation. I open my eyes and see others doing the same.

'It is time for dinner', says our kindly host. The dining-table is set in European fashion for four persons, but only the son of Mr. R. keeps us company, his wife, according to Hindu custom, is serving us. After dinner my host, having shown me my bed-room, advised me to put my cot half out on the verandah, so that my head would be outside to feel a little breeze during the hot night.

Next day before evening, accompanied by the son of Mr. R., I reached my steamer and, after having taken leave of my kind host, I left the soil of Ceylon. The steamer moved slowly out of the harbour. I climbed the highest deck to look once more on Colombo with its innumerable fading lights.

A big ship with British migrants was passing ours. I saw dancing pairs under the waterproof roof of the upper deck and heard the noisy music of jazz.

And a long phosphorescent wake was visible on the water behind our steamer.

CHAPTER XLV

On the Ocean

The weather was marvellous during the whole of the journey. Windy days when the steamer was tossed about were very few. Clear blue sunny sky was our portion all the time. In a few days we should be crossing the Equator, hence the position of the Sun is changing; it is nearing North about noon, then it seems to stay in the very middle of the sky vertically over our heads. The further we go, the more our conception of 'the South' changes to geographical 'North'.

There is only one class on the steamer, so its corners and nooks are accessible to all the passengers. Comfortable and spacious halls for reading and writing tempt me to write a few more pages in my Diary, although the real journey to India ended a week ago. When will come my next?

The monotonous days of this return journey are filled with meditation. I see the same world, the same people round me, with their worries and hopes, with their good and bad qualities. And yet, no, it is not true, the world has changed tremendously if compared with that of my previous years. Instead of an alien and seldom friendly entity, a picture of the whole is now seen, but as if it were on a somewhat dimmed and hazy film which is unrolled before my eyes by an invisible yet quite real power. In this film my own person plays the same role as millions of other so-called 'human beings'. In days of old I was continually identifying my-self with my 'ego' and could not think about it otherwise than as the subject, but now I have learned that there are other states of consciousness in which one is free from such a limited and condi-tioned material existence. I have learned that there is such a thing as true freedom which is real happiness too. The spectre of death has no power over it. What is the true basis of this new state of consciousness? I think that the key to all these higher states is the

183

capacity to look objectively upon our personalities and be able to say: '*I know where is the Self and where the non-Self*'.

Practice in everyday life consists of a growing awareness that forms are not real and only that which has no form has reality. But reasoning cannot create such a conception—on the contrary—the stoppage of reasoning can do so, and this is far more difficult than any kind of intellectual exertion. It seems to me that there is a law according to which, once we leave the realm of thought and stop the functioning of brain-mind, the new state of consciousness independent of thought must necessarily dawn. To many people this very possibility may seem absurd, for they instinctively cling to the unfortunate—or perhaps only wrongly expressed—words of Descartes: 'Cogito, ergo sum', 'I think, therefore I am'.

But there is certainly a power in us which is able to control the mind-brain and guide it just as one guides the movements of the fingers of one's hand. The secret undoubtedly lies in this capacity of 'stopping'. In the beginning it is a hard task, it requires effort and struggle, but soon it becomes a source of happiness. Can it be acquired without the assistance of a Master, of a being who has achieved these results and now is a source of real peace radiating in all directions? I do not know, I am not sure. The great majority of Hindus believe that it is not possible.

I know that no problem should now worry me. The very existence of problems, says Maharshi, proves our spiritual ignorance. It is quite true, for the very putting of a problem means an attempt to bring down reality to the mental level, and this is equal to the effort of attempting to draw water with a sieve. Even an ordinary vessel cannot hold a subtle ethereal substance. Alas, the understanding of all this comes only when we have been able to transcend the limitations of the mind-brain; before this is achieved it is only the repetition of empty words.

*   *   *

I am sitting alone in a corner of the saloon. The sun is setting, its great red disc is plunging into the ocean, half of it has already disappeared in the silvery water at the horizon. There is peace in Nature and peace in me. Peace is bliss. For any movement proves the necessity of change, and where there is change there is *no perfection*, for *perfection* does not need any *change*.

I know that this peace in me is neither final nor permanent, it may be only a reflection, but the very existence of a reflection proves that the archetype is there. And in this certainty lies a power which will lead us to the goal and make It attainable.

Like sufferings and pleasures which, belonging to the past thereby lose all reality and simply do not exist any more, so every state which is not perfect must vanish. The past and future exist only in the imagination. Created by our mind, which is only the process of thinking, they must perish with its creator. That is why the stopping of the stream of thoughts gives us the first glimpse and touch of unchangeable reality.

*   *   *

I have made peace with the world. Let peace be also its lot. When good and evil cease, unchanging peace will come. When the changing vibrations have no place in our consciousness, we shall return to peace which is all. Peace exists always and everywhere, but the unspiritualized consciousness of human beings, who in their ignorance believe in their separate existences, do not see this peace. I have had the privilege of seeing what a human being who attains this peace is like.

I have seen eyes which told me without words about this peace. I know that I shall never forget—it is absolutely impossible—what the light in Maharshi's eyes conveyed. And in spite of the fact that the physical distance between me and the place where they are still shining is growing every minute; in spite of the circumstance that soon those eyes will close to the visible world, their speech will live in the hearts of all those who have once seen and accepted their light. The highest power that shines through Its chosen ones will never be exhausted. Let this power be blessed in our hearts. Were It to manifest in all Its inexpressible might it would blind us and burn us to ashes in our frailty. Yet It looks at us with love and kindness through the eyes of Those who, through Their incredible effort have merged Their consciousness in It, achieving *union* for ever.

CHAPTER XLVI

The Light is Shining

Maharshi has left this world. But those who have understood his mission, his message and his teachings have not remained orphans. He still lives in their hearts and his influence will increase as they advance towards truth. They do not mourn the departure of the beloved Master and Friend. The same light is still shining on his pupils scattered all over the world, for it is also the very core of their own being.

When many years ago one of his pupils said that he wanted to remain in the Ashram at any cost, to be always in the physical vicinity of 'Bhagavan', Maharshi answered:

'The Spiritual Being dwelling in you is the Real Bhagavan, that is what you have to realize'.

Can there be any loftier spiritual conception? In discovering our own real Self we discover our beloved master at the same time. And there is no other way. This Self is *All*, and nothing exists beyond and apart from *It*. So there is no use searching for anything else but the Self, all else is illusion.

*　　*　　*

In a quiet peaceful corner of India near the last resting-place of the Sage of Arunachala, the remaining disciples and devotees of the Master are gathering every day. They sing the same hymns which were sung in the temple hall during his lifetime. Silence reigns in its purity all round and in the hearts of those who were privileged to have witnessed Maharshi's mission. My Indian friends in their letters call the present state of Maharshi 'Mahasamadhi', which can be translated as 'the great union' or 'the great and final contemplation' which expresses at least in part the beautiful Sanscrit term.

In spite of the fact that a dense and heavy darkness still envelops mankind in this critical stage of its evolution, it is an undeniable fact that real spiritual beauty and greatness irresistibly attract many of us, and this is the best proof of the future possibilities hidden in all human beings. It was always so. It will always be so.

The Great Teachers who came down here to shed light on the path of humanity have always had round Them a group to be a fertile soil into which the blessed seeds of true wisdom could fall, not to be dried up, but to germinate. The phenomenon of Maharshi is one more proof that the ways of providence are adapted to the stages of evolution reached by mankind in every era. Now, when the minds of the dwellers on our planet have become somewhat more developed as compared with those of past ages, at least so far as the mass of humanity is concerned—I do not speak of special individuals—spiritual teaching had to be given in an adequate form.

When many religions and sects were quarrelling with each other, there was need for a presentation of truth which would transcend all the enclosing walls of particular faiths. This was given by Maharshi. His teachings can be accepted by any man sincerely seeking God and truth independently of the religion in which he has been reared. There is moreover the fact that in the light of Maharshi's teachings, the truths contained in the sacred scriptures of every religion can be easily understood and their seeming contradictions cease to exist for seekers of truth.

Self-knowledge, according to the experimental methods of the Great Indian Rishi leads us to a religious synthesis. We see that the Buddha, the Christ, and minor, or rather less known, Messengers all speak about the same reality, only the outward way of presenting It may vary in accordance with the needs of the epoch and the possibilities of human understanding. All fanaticism and intolerance which are such great obstacles in our search for God are then dropped.

It is from these two plagues that political and social fanaticisms and despotisms are born and their devastating effects are seen in our own times.

Maharshi touches the true cause of all the crimes and misfortunes afflicting humanity. He says clearly:

'All sins and wickedness are born from the false human notion that causes people to identify themselves with their bodies. There is no sin in which the motive of selfishness and this identification with the body cannot be discovered'.

It is obvious that all evil can be traced to this cause. Similarly the opposite assertion:

'I am not this body, I am the Eternal Spirit dwelling temporarily in this vehicle of flesh'.

radically uproots all evil motives.

That is the essence of Maharshi's Message, the essence of the teachings of *One of the last Great Rishis* of India, so far as I was able to understand it.

CHAPTER XLVII

Samadhi

After this diary covering my stay in India was finished under its present title *In Days of Great Peace*, some friends who read the manuscript raised the question of Samadhi. They asked: 'What is this state? How can one reach it? What is it like? How long can it last? What may be regarded as its forerunner? What happens to our physical-mental consciousness when we are in it?' and so on. They also asked me to explain what path can lead us to Samadhi, or simply what have we to do to experience this state.

I can only answer that the safest way is to study the teachings of those in whom Samadhi is the normal state of consciousness. There are such saints in every religion, there are such Great Rishis in India. Only those who know this state in all its fullness can talk about it with competence and without personal colouring.

There are two states of Samadhi: one is the temporary Samadhi —it means a spiritual ecstasy appearing spontaneously, sporadically, or even as a result of a deliberate effort, but lasting only for a brief time, after which one returns to the 'normal' state of consciousness which bears only some traces of the experienced ecstasy, some reflection of it, as it were, just like sunbeams reflected in a jar of water. This kind is experienced in many of its various forms by saints, yogis, and pupils of different spiritual schools.

Of course all I can say about Samadhi will concern only its 'temporary form'. But this may lead to the lasting and absolute Samadhi, which is reached only by Men made perfect, who appear like meteors on the spiritual firmament of humanity. Yet as we know nothing about this supreme state—called by Sri Ramana Maharshi 'natural state' or 'Sahaja Samadhi'—we are quite unable to discuss it. It would be as useless as to try to solve an equation with too many unknowns.

One of the characteristics of this 'natural state' is its continuity, its uninterruptedness. Maharshi achieved it in the second half of his life. When we read his biography—*Self-Realization*' by Narasimha Swami and similar works—we note that before 1930 he often spoke about himself: 'Then I was not in Samadhi', but after that year he speaks of it as a normal, permanent, 'natural state', without interruptions, without any place for the physical-mental consciousness. When this state is reached it makes no difference whether one speaks or is silent, whether one moves or sleeps, or performs any visible action, as consciousness never descends to the level which is called 'normal' by us.

I purposely do not use the Indian Yogic terminology, for it would only make the comprehension of the subject more difficult for those who are unacquainted with it, and Indians will understand even without the classical terms.

The state of temporary Samadhi—the only one about which we can speak—necessitates, while it lasts, a certain limitation of the physical functions. Some have to sit in complete immobility so that the physical body is in a kind of torpor; the breathing sometimes almost stops, or spontaneously follows a special rhythm. I am not speaking here about those who practice meditation with the purpose of reaching Samadhi, and deliberately adopt certain *breathing exercises* to achieve this purpose; but these practices are not recommended by the Great Rishis. Other people plunge into a deep meditation or rapture, and for the time being lose all sense of physical consciousness, or else see all the outer world as through a mist or in a dream.

Many deliberately seek the same surroundings in which they were once able to experience such an ecstasy, thereby hoping to reach the same state again. Others pray for it or ask the assistance of their Master. But it is the achievement which matters and not the circumstances and surroundings in which it takes place.

It was asked: 'How can we know that we have really reached the state of Samadhi or spiritual ecstasy?'

Normally we know by our own experience—common to all human beings—only two states of consciousness: the *waking* and the *sleeping* or dreaming state. Let us analyze them briefly, so that afterwards, we may be able to approach the *third* one intelligently. It is an undeniable fact that in sleep our experiences are somewhat like, and at the same time very different from, the waking state. Sleep also differs with different people. With some it is very vague, uncertain, misty. Others speak of having in it clear, definite and 'real' experiences. It probably depends on the brain and nervous system and upon the general development of the individual. But when we wake up, we generally regard our dreams of the night as unreal, and we are not inclined during our waking state to endow them with any special meaning. If such dreams are unpleasant, we say: 'At last it is over. Fortunately it was *only a dream*'. It means that the immediately higher state *excludes* the lower and makes it quite unimportant and insignificant in our eyes. If while reading these lines, we clearly grasp this fact, it will be easier for us to acquire a mental understanding of the state of Samadhi.

Its relation to the waking state is just the same as the waking is to the sleeping one.

If we grasp this idea, many chapters of this book will become clearer, and we shall understand the teachings of Maharshi more easily.

Would you, in your waking state, meditate on what you have seen in your dream? For instance, if you were 'killed' in your dream, could it have any influence on your daily life? Or if you dream of taking a meal, can it satisfy your hunger in your waking state? Can you imagine it? We simply deny all reality to dreams when we are in our 'normal' waking state. And *we are right*. Let us take a step further. From the next higher state, called Samadhi, just in the same way our earthly waking state is seen *like a dream*. *And this is the criterion* we must find when we ask: 'How can we know that we have reached the transcendental state?'

It seems that Samadhi has three phases:

The First—when we feel it is approaching. In this state we can still move and talk as usual. We can compare it to early twilight before sunrise.

The Second can be compared to the midday when the sun stands high in the sky. Then the mental and physical functions decline, they become dreamy, and *reality* alone, independent of all form and condition, dawns upon and illumines our being. We then *know Who we are*, we do not identify ourselves any more with our personalities, we are above and beyond them. We breathe freedom, bliss and wisdom.

The Third—which comes immediately after our 'coming back' from Samadhi, is like the second twilight, this time preceding 'sunset'. We still feel in ourselves its last rays, we still clearly remember the *light*, but its vivid reality gradually fades away when we return to our 'normal' consciousness, the 'waking' state. But the remembrance of Samadhi is never completely lost. We are still unable to stay in it permanently, due to our imperfect spiritual development, but henceforth we *know* irrefutably that this state exists, that it *is* in truth, the only reality. After experiencing Samadhi even once we are different beings.

It is interesting to note that this state has its own range of vibrations, extremely subtle and powerful. They influence our surroundings; we can easily observe their effect on people when we experience, however imperfectly, this state ourselves. When, being at the very threshold of the Samadhi sunrise, we talk to others, or when we just emerge from the Samadhi sunset, we can notice that people are behaving—probably unconsciously—somewhat differently, and addressing us in another tone than usual, although from without they can see nothing save our 'normal' ordinary persons. But each one has his own Samadhi deep in his heart in a latent state, which one day will reveal itself. Thus this 'dormant' germ of the Spirit responds to the vibrations of the spirit awakened.

We may now understand what a tremendous help it is for everyone to be in the presence of a Master who has achieved the fullness of Samadhi, with whom this state is normal and continuous. This spiritual 'magnetism' is the most powerful element which awakens the pupil from the slumbering of matter into the

N

light of the real. If you grasp this point you may better understand the experiences of those who have been in Maharshi's presence.

I do not exactly know by what law the words of the Master, when read or meditated upon, are also most helpful in the awakening of our Spirit. The places where he dwelt, conversations with those who knew him and were his pupils, also assists us in the opening and broadening of our consciousness and the enlargement of its horizons. I am stating this as a fact, although I am unable to explain its basis or the whys and wherefores of its working.

Some people have experienced Samadhi under the influence of a deep emotion or rapture. The well-known Saint of India, Sri Ramakrishna often fell into the trance of Samadhi under the influence of an outer impulse. Once in the Zoological Gardens of Calcutta he went into Samadhi at the sight of a lion; and afterwards explained that he saw in this kingly animal the reflection of the power of the Most High, and one instant of this contemplation was enough to carry him out of the normal consciousness into the higher state of Samadhi.

The contemplation of mighty mountains or the vast expanse of the sea, and other forms of the beauty and power of Nature, also help us considerably to leave our 'physical sleep' for the higher state. Can anyone who has read the life of Saint Francis of Assisi and of other Saints of a contemplative and devotional temperament, fail to notice the same phenomenon in Sri Ramakrishna's life?

But do we really need many examples from different biographies? Are we not aware that some lofty thoughts and sublime inner flights can be awakened in our own hearts when we sit quietly on the seashore looking at the splendour of a sunset, or when we contemplate a vast panorama from a high hill? We may raise this feeling to a much higher potency in our imagination, add to it 'stillness of the mind' and purity of the heart, and— we may *not be far from the understanding of our goal*. Through music, songs, mantras, incantations, one can also obtain the same results; that is why they were introduced in all the religions of the world.

Samadhi is a state of absolute Bliss. One can say that tiny elements of Samadhi are present in every pure and intense bliss that we experience even in our ordinary daily lives; however small these 'drops of nectar' may be, their essence is the same as the ecstasy of Samadhi. Wherever, under any impulse, we can escape from our narrow personality and forget 'the dream of our waking state' the germ of Samadhi is present.

But no one can reach this lofty state through *curiosity* or the so-called *'passion for knowledge'*. No amount of effort can help you in this respect if such be your motive. Vain attempt! Samadhi cannot be encased in the narrow boundaries of the mind, for its very characteristic is the transcendence of all mental levels. Do not deceive yourself by saying that you would like to study this state 'scientifically', for this would be similar to trying to take water with a sieve.

It is *your motive*, the *purpose* you want to achieve, that alone is the factor deciding success. Only intuition can guide you. Only when you are ripe for the wholehearted desire to exchange all that is transitory in yourself for the permanent and eternal, *when the Eternal becomes more important for you than all the seeming 'reality' of the visible world*, will you be capable and ready for the great effort, and then only will the necessary *assistance* be given to you.

Some adepts of spiritual science say that Samadhi is stronger than death, that one cannot die in this state, for all physical life is then in a kind of suspension. That is, according to them, the basis of the belief that some yogis who practice certain forms of Samadhi can live hundreds—sometimes thousands—of years. On the other hand, cases are known of yogis who have left this world by not returning to their normal consciousness from the state of Samadhi.

*   *   *

We can find much light on the subject of higher states of consciousness in the following books: *Varieties of Religious Experiences* a classic by Prof. W. James, *A Search in Secret India* and other works by Paul Brunton, and the incomparable *Maha Yoga* by

'Who', published by Ramanasramam at Tiruvannamalai; it is the work of one of the most advanced pupils of Maharshi and contains his teachings *in extenso*.

The path is always open. It depends only on you whether you will direct your steps towards it or not. But remember always that those who are treading it will certainly welcome you with joy. Some people think that the physical death of the Master makes the path for novices impossible. Nothing is further from the truth. We cannot discuss this here. I can only advise you to read the very valuable book *Ramana Maharshi and the Path of Self-Knowledge* (Rider & Co.) by Arthur Osborne, who spent some time in the immediate presence of Maharshi.

CHAPTER XLVIII

The Last Message

Now you have nearly finished this book. Some, yawning, will put it on the shelf; some will meditate over it, will think of the unknown disciple and his Master. An ancient occult tradition says that everything about spiritual matters is best read at least seven times. And only at the seventh reading will the student enter into the realm revealed.

I have read the little book *The Voice of the Silence* by H. P. Blavatsky at least seven times seven, and with each reading more light poured from its pages. Similarly with *Viveka-Chudamani* by Sri Sankaracharya. The method is proved sound and practical. If you will give the necessary time and perseverance, the silence through Vichara will stop your restless mind, and the real will manifest itself. Do not try to hasten the process. Perhaps this book was written for you, not for the outer 'you' but the real *you*. For *you* and I are one.

Often questions arise which may be anticipated. Let us answer some of them.

Is the Path shown by one of the last Great Rishis appropriate for you? If when reading or listening to the teachings and lives of spiritual geniuses whom we call saints and sages, your heart melts and you feel that the invisible spiritual current draws you in, then know that it may be a call for you. Let us not extinguish those delicate movements of the spiritual flame which is hidden deep below the layers of our personality. When in such moments everything in you melts into a mighty desire to step after *Him*, after this still unknown, but already beloved Master, then in fact *He* is calling you. It is the only way He can call—from within your being, not from without. If you see, as in the brightness of a lightning flash the whole unreality of the visible world, including your temporary, limited form, called till now you, then prepare yourself for the Great Pilgrimage. Forget then the past and the future, the petty aims of your transient physical existence; only the eternal, unchanging, glorious present has henceforth to concern you.

Everything apart from *It* is your false self—your vampire-like ego, your Maya—the realm of the unreal. If an irresistible desire to enter on the path does not arise in you, if you cannot realize what this path is really about, then it is clear the time is not yet ripe for you. The ordinary ways of life are more appropriate. To be honest, good and full of sympathy is a necessary step towards the Direct Path which will reveal itself in due course.

I do not wish to conceal difficulties which will surely be encountered on the path. Therefore you should know that to create evil by thoughts, deeds or feelings when once on the path will lead to danger and catastrophe. So said the Lord Buddha:

'Cease doing evil; learn to do good; purify your own heart'.

Those are the qualities which develop in the disciple when he really engages in the Vichara. The Vichara itself creates these virtues. That is logical. When you cease to recognise your ego, where will be the motive for doing evil? When the ego disappears, all evil goes with it.

The fulfilment of the above three commandments produces a saint. And saintship is the first real step to liberation or self-realization. Do not doubt that statement. There are more Saints about at the present time than many people suppose. And they do not all wear monk's robes and have shaven heads. They may look like average men. A saint can only be recognized if he chooses to reveal himself. And his ways of life apparently do not differ much from those of others. Only an intimate contact with him will reveal his saintship.

A wise Yogi once said:

'If a flower has honey the bee will find it. It is not the flower which seeks the bee'.

So it will be with your entry on the path and into discipleship of a Master. As the bee finds the flower, so you will find Him. Sri Ramana Maharshi said to his intimate disciples:

'There is no alternative for you but to accept the world as unreal, if you are seeking Truth and Truth alone. For the simple reason, that unless you give up the idea that the world is real, your mind will always be after it. If you take the appearance to be real, you will never know the Real Itself, although it is the Real alone that exists'.

This saying is of great importance to the seeker. How does a disciple realize that condition? It comes gradually, but irresistibly, as you Vichara proceeds. Practically, you feel as if you were separated from your visible, physical form. Walking, speaking and performing different activities you begin to feel that you are beyond and above the acting form. It is a wonderful feeling of freedom and bliss. No doubts or fears exist. These moments are rare in the beginning, it is true, but in the course of progress they come more and more frequently. These are the first rays of the light of your true Self, which is happiness itself.

Years ago, when meditating about my Master, I conceived Him to be a lord of bliss. And when I saw him, I gave myself to him for ever. From that time on the world had no more appeal. I lost my little self reflected in the conventional life.

Scriptures say: '*Naked man must stand before the Most High*'.

Everywhere we find guide posts on the path. By giving up everything we find all. The paradox is realized, the mystical Truth is proved.

If we are unhappy it is our own error. Therefore do not believe that there are circumstances or conditions which are responsible for the darkness within us. It is the ego-mind which begets this lie. For no limitations concern the real *you*.

It is difficult at first to realize our separateness from the visible form in the state of sleep. For innumerable ages of existence in separate forms we acquired the habit of merging our consciousness in darkness when asleep. But as the Vichara proceeds it will enlighten even this bastion of darkness in due course.

When you dive into the sea, you take off your clothes beforehand. When you dive into the Self in Samadhi you must put aside your outer self. The thoughts and emotions must be discarded, at least temporarily, before Samadhi can be experienced. Many books could be written about these experiences, but they would be of little use without the practice of Vichara. And then everything comes of its own accord. As Maharshi says:

'Knowing the Self by means of the Vichara you will find your Master within yourself'.

Now it may be clear why disciples of the Master are always conscious of His presence. Every devoted seeker will find him in his own heart, though he has not seen him in his physical form. And this invisible presence is as potent as was his physical one.

Nevertheless there is a strange power and inspiration in the pictures of Maharshi. Were it not so he would never have permitted them to be made.

May the grace of the Great Being to whom this book is dedicated, enlighten your endeavours.

CHAPTER XLIX

Epilogue

The sad news of Sri Ramana Maharshi's departure from the physical body soon reached me and his other devotees scattered throughout the world. I do not wish to praise, or compare with other Masters, the Great Being at whose feet the Almighty allowed me to abide. For how could we, from our lower level of consciousness exactly describe the being whose mission was to give us something of his infinite light? Adequately to assess his greatness, one must at least be on the same level of spiritual glory. All that I can do, is to try to convey what I found in my own heart when I received the news.

The light from those luminous eyes of Sri Maharshi was for ever engraved on my memory before leaving the Ashram. And now—the account of his death lies before me. Does it mean that those eyes cannot radiate their silent initiation any more? That would be ridiculous. I know this light is not a material one, though it was conveyed through a material body. This is a mystery but not a paradox. In my heart I found no urge to discover that mystery through the mind. I felt that the fact was so, even though inexplicable to the thinking process. So his death did not deprive me of his reality.

I was quietly sitting as if in preparation for meditation. But this time the usual process changed. Perhaps He saw that the human heart, not yet free from all its weaknesses, sometimes needs some consolation. And then, instead of a void, the well-known and beloved picture arose before me.

There were most mysterious and inspiring evenings at the Ashram when the beautiful hymn 'In Praise of the Lord of the Universe' was sung in the hall. Sri Maharshi evidently loved the hymn, for there would appear a peculiar expression of other than human beatitude and delight on His face. I felt that the hearts of those who were present in that blissful hour of the evening contemplation were deeply tuned to it. Perhaps His penetrating inner sight saw the beneficial process in us, and His silent blessing was the answer.

How can we fathom the unfathomable? And now, as if still in the temple hall with all those others, I once again listened to the same beautiful melody heard before with my outer ears. It was as if I reviewed a film. And there was no sadness any more. It could not be otherwise! The true legacy of the Master could never be less than joy, this sublime and silent joy of being, untroubled by the waves of the surrounding illusory world or Maya. This was His peace which He bequeathed to us.

Later on letters came from devotees in other countries. My distant friends each gave their own accounts of how the tragic news affected them. They tried their best to console themselves and me, by saying that the physical departure of the Master could not break our spiritual link with Him. And yet the ink in the last paragraphs of such letters was often blurred as if with tears.

It is said that love was the force which created the universe. Perhaps it is. But to me the force of such unselfish and radiant love as His, is just that power which purifies our hearts, when all other methods prove useless.

Neither occult training nor any other method, can give the disciple the true peace which the Master gives.

Sri Maharshi was a centre of love to his disciples. He left us his love, and where else in the world could be found a purifying power such as this, to bring peace to our hearts?

The anniversaries of the Mahasamadhi of Sri Maharshi will come one after another. And some year will see the last one for me on this earth.

But at the last moment He will be with me, as with everyone of you who knew Him, and you who yearn to know Him, if you keep to the end, His legacy of love.

*   *   *

Those who feel an intuitive attraction to the Direct Path of the

Great Rishi Ramana, as experienced by the writer and described —to a certain extent—in this book, may be interested in the following steps which came later for the author.

Now, when I am looking back from the perspective of a few years, I see that the process which began in Bhagavan's Ashram is uninterruptedly going ahead, changing the whole inner structure of a man.

Many outer things, such as worldly conditions and karmic ties, which before were considered as obstacles, are now becoming as unreal as a passing mist. The inner experiences are now taking a more steady and controllable shape, and losing their former unpredictable and rather sporadic character; because they are now directed by an irresistible Will, which mysteriously is—*at the same time*—both *inside and outside of man*.

The thinking process as it was in past years has disappeared and cannot be found again. Instead, in its place has come the awareness of the perpetual cosmic current of mind; but it is flowing *apart* from my consciousness, except when I am selecting what I need from it.

This means, that the formerly invincible compulsion of constant thinking has gone for ever, and in its place is a newly-born and quite *natural* tendency *to remain in the silent shrine of the heart or self*, where no thought or emotion dare to enter. There is no effort needed any more as truly predicted by the Master in His teachings, and no exercise has to be performed as in the past.

Basically, the inner experiences described throughout this book are by no means deprived of their sense. They have lost only their spontaneous nature, having deepened and become well entrenched in the same visible outer shell—the body.

There is no purpose in delving into them here; for they would be quite incomprehensible to anyone who has not yet lived what has been described. The process of ripening is rather an automatic one; all 'plannings' and calculations for the 'future', together with all hopes, fears and griefs belong to the dead past.

Sri Maharshi says: 'He that has earned the grace of the Guru shall undoubtedly be saved and never forsaken, just as the prey that has fallen into the tiger's jaws will never be allowed to escape'. In other words, once the path is found it cannot be lost any more, no matter how many lives still lie before us.

The more my physical shell wears out in the course of the quickly passing years and heads for its natural end, the firmer the inner reality (so inexpressible in words) takes command of my being, as a kind of unbroken consciousness, extending further and deeper.

A verse from St. John comes to mind:

'That which is born of flesh is flesh; and that which is born of the Spirit is Spirit'.

Imagination, visions, and other products of the mind's activity do not exist on the Direct Path. Reality excludes all illusions. Instead, only what could be called the illimitable bliss, the fulfilment of our deepest and most pure hopes and spiritual strivings, can follow us on that path.

It is my firm conviction, that in this world at the present time, there are still many who would be able to enter on this sublime path, the unique direct highway to the absolute. And it is for them, and them alone, that this book has been written. I am stretching out my hand to them. Will they accept it?

CHAPTER L

Appendix—Matter for Meditation

In order to train our minds properly to approach spiritual axioms, meditation is necessary. The immortal treatise *Viveka-Chudamani* (The Crest Jewel of Wisdom) by Sri Sankaracharya is a fruitful source. It is incomparable evidence of the heights to which the human spirit can soar, and is useful as a subject for meditation.

From meditation on these verses—not only reading them— there arises an appropriate attitude of mind.

This attitude is equivalent to the purification and making sensitive of our as yet imperfect organ of cognition of spirit.

The conceptions embedded in the teachings of Sri Sankaracharya are not contrary to mental logic, but they are the ultimate extension of it in the unconditioned truth in ourselves.

The verses given here are from the translation by Mohini M. Chatterji.

For all those not yet acquainted with the age-old conceptions of Vedanta, these few extracts may serve as a necessary preparation.

At least they help towards an understanding of how a human being, seeking spiritual Light here and now, may proceed.

1. I prostrate myself before the true teacher—before him who is revealed by the conclusions of all systems of Vedantic philosophy, but is himself unknown, Govinda the supreme bliss.

4. One who, having with difficulty acquired a human incarnation and in that manhood a knowledge of the scriptures, through delusions does not labour for emancipation, is a suicide destroying himself in trying to attain illusive objects.

6. He may study the scriptures, propitiate the gods (by sacrifices), perform religious ceremonies or offer devotion to the gods, yet he will not attain salvation even during the succession of a hundred Brahma-yugas except by the knowledge of union with the spirit.

8. Therefore the wise man strives for his salvation, having renounced his desire for the enjoyment of external objects, and betakes himself to a true and great teacher and accepts his teaching with an unshaken soul.

9. And by the practice of right discrimination attained by the path of Yoga he rescues the soul—the soul drowned in the sea of conditioned existence.

11. Actions are for the purification of the heart, not for the attainment of the real substance. The substance can be attained by right discrimination, but not by any amount of Karma.

32. Among the instruments of emancipation the supreme is devotion. Meditation upon the true form of the real Self is said to be devotion.

33. Some say devotion is meditation on the nature of one's Atman. He who possesses all these qualifications is one who is fit to know the true nature of Atman.

39. The great and peaceful ones live regenerating the world like the coming of spring, and after having themselves crossed the ocean of embodied existence, help those who try to do the same thing, without personal motives.

40. This desire is spontaneous, since the natural tendency of great souls is to remove the suffering of others just as the ambrosia-rayed (moon) of itself cools the earth heated by the harsh rays of the sun.

46. There is an effectual means for the destruction of birth and re-birth by which, crossing the ocean of changing life, thou wilt attain to supreme bliss.

53. Sons and others are capable of discharging a father's debts; but no one except oneself can remove (his own) bondage.

54. Others can remove the pain (caused by the weight of) burdens placed on the head, but the pain (that arises) from hunger and the like cannot be removed except by oneself.

61. If the supreme truth remains unknown, the study of the scriptures is fruitless; even if the supreme truth is known the study

of the scriptures is useless (the study of the letter alone is useless, the spirit must be sought out by intuition).

62. In a labyrinth of words the mind is lost like a man in a thick forest, therefore with great efforts must be learned the truth about oneself from him who knows the truth.

63. Of what use are the Vedas to him who has been bitten by the snake of ignorance? (Of what use are) scriptures, incantations, or any medicine except the medicine of supreme knowledge?

64. Disease is never cured by (pronouncing) the name of medicine without taking it; liberation is not achieved by the (pronunciation of the) word Brahman without direct perception.

66. Without the conquest of enemies, without command of the treasure of a vast country, by the mere words 'I am a king', it is impossible to become one.

86. He who lives only to nourish his own body, is like one who crosses a river on an alligator thinking it to be a log of wood.

87. For one desirous of liberation, desires pertaining to the body, etc., lead to the great death; he who is free from such desires is alone fit to gain liberation.

92. Know that this gross body, on which depend all the external manifestations of *the purusa*, is but like the house of the householder.

128. Who during waking, dreaming, and dreamless slumber knows the mind and its functions which are goodness and its absence—this is the Self.

134. This unmanifested spiritual consciousness begins to manifest like the dawn in the pure heart, and shining like the mid-day sun in the 'cave of wisdom' illuminating whole universe.

160. Full of misery, covered with flesh, full of filth, full of sin, how can it be the knower? The Self is different from this.

161. The deluded man considers the Self to be the mass of skin, flesh, fat, bones and filth. The man of discrimination knows the essential form of self, which is the supreme truth, to be without these as characteristic marks.

166. Because the false conviction that the self is merely the

IN DAYS OF GREAT PEACE

body, is the seed producing pain in the form of birth and the rest, efforts must be made to abandon that idea; the attraction towards material existence will then cease to exist.

175. Having produced attachment to the body and all other objects, it thus binds the individual as an animal is bound by a rope, afterwards having produced aversion to these as if to poison, that *manas* itself frees him from bondage.

176. Therefore the *manas* is the cause of the bondage of this individual and also of its liberation. The manas when stained by passion is the cause of bondage, and of liberation when pure, devoid of passion and ignorance.

178. In the forest land of objects wanders the great tiger named *manas*; pure men desirous of liberation do not go there.

220. The fool, having seen the image of the sun in the water of the jar, thinks it is the sun. So an ignorant man seeing the reflection of the Logos in any of the *upadhis* (vehicles) takes it to be the real self.

221. As the wise man looks at the sun itself and not the jar, the water, or the reflection; so also the wise man looks towards the self-illumined *atman* through which the three (*upadhis*) are manifested.

222, 223. Thus it is that the individual, abandoning the body, the intellect and the reflection of consciousness, becomes sinless, passionless and deathless by knowing the self-illuminated *atman*, which is the seer, which is itself the eternal knowledge, different from reality as well as unreality, eternal, all pervading, supremely subtle, devoid of within and without, the only one, in the centre of wisdom.

229. By reason of ignorance this universe appears multiform, but in reality all this is *Brahman* (which remains), when all defective mental states have been rejected.

235. The Lord, the knower of all objects in their reality, has declared, 'I am not distinct from them nor are they distinct from me'.

236. If this universe is a reality, it should be perceived in dream-

less slumber. Since, however, nothing is perceived (in that condition) it is as unreal as dreams.

240. When all the differences created by *maya* (illusion) have been rejected, (there remains) a self-illumined something which is eternal, fixed, without stain, immeasurable, without form, unmanifested, without name, indestructible.

241. The wise know that as the supreme truth which is absolute consciousness, in which are united the knower, the known and the knowledge, infinite and unchangeable.

271. Having given up following the way of the world, the body, or the scriptures, remove the erroneous conception that *Atman* is *Non-atman*.

274. As by mixture with water and by friction, sandal-wood emits an excellent odour, removing all bad smells; so divine aspiration becomes manifest when external desire is washed away.

276. The aspiration towards *atman* is stifled by the net of unspiritual desires, for by constant devotion to *atman* they are destroyed, and divine aspiration becomes manifest.

285. So long as the notion 'I am this body' is not completely abandoned, control yourself with great concentration, and with great effort remove the erroneous conception that Non-spirit is Spirit.

298. Abandon the notion of 'I' in family, clan, name, form and state of life, which all depend on this physical body and also having abandoned the properties of the *linga s'arira*, such as the feeling of being the actor and the rest—become the essential form which is absolute bliss.

316. Vasana, nourished by these two,* produces the changing life of the ego. Means for the destruction of this triad always, under all circumstances (should be sought).

317. By everywhere, in every way, looking upon everything as Brahman, and by strengthening the perception of the (one) reality this triad will disappear.

---

*Thought and external action.

318. By the extinction of action, comes the extinction of anxious thought, from this (latter) the extinction of *vasana*. The final extinction of *vasana* is liberation—that is also called *jivanmukti*.

327. The mind directed towards objects of sense determines their qualities (and thus becomes attracted by them); from this determination arises desire, and from desire human action.

328. From that comes separation from the real self; one thus separated retrogrades. There is not seen the reascent but the destruction of the fallen one. Therefore abandon thoughts (about sense-objects), the cause of all evils.

329. Therefore for one possessed of discrimination, knowing Brahman in *samadhi*, there is no death other than from negligence. He who is absorbed in (the real) self, achieves the fullest success; hence be heedful and self-controlled.

330. He who while living realizes unity (with the supreme), does so also when devoid of the body. For him who is conscious of even the slightest differentiation there is fear—so says the Yajur-Veda.

368. The first gate of yoga is the control of speech, then non-acceptance (of anything and all), absence of expectation, absence of desire and uninterrupted devotion to the one (reality).

376. For him who is possessed of excessive dispassion there is *samadhi*; for him in *samadhi* there is unwavering spiritual perception. For him who has perceived the essential reality there is liberation, and for the liberated atman there is realization of eternal bliss.

385. Regard the indestructible and all-pervading Atman, freed from all the *upadhis*—body, senses, vitality, mind, egotism and the rest—produced by ignorance as *mahakasa* (great space).

389. The atman is Brahma, the atman is Visnu, the atman is Indra, the atman is Siva, the atman is the whole of this universe; besides Atman there is nothing.

390. The atman is within, the atman is without, the atman is before; the atman is behind, the atman is in the south, the atman is in the north, the atman is also above and below.

398. On the removal of all phenomenal attributes imposed upon the self, the true self is (found to be) the supreme, non-dual, and actionless Brahman.

419. The gain of the yogi who has attained perfection is the enjoyment of perpetual bliss in the atman.

448. By the knowledge that I (the Logos) am Brahman, the Karma acquired in a thousand millions of kalpas is extinguished, as is the Karma of dream life on awakening.

450. Having realized his real self as space, without attachment and indifferent (to worldly concerns), he never clings to (becomes united with) anything whatsoever by future karma.

458. Similarly he who ever abides in the atman and thus in *Parabrahman*, sees nothing else. Eating, sleeping, etc., are to a wise man but as the recollection of objects seen in dream.

482. Through the realization of the atman with Brahman, (my) understanding is utterly lost and mental activity has vanished. I know neither this nor that, nor what this bliss is, its extent, nor its limit.

483. The greatness of *parabrahman*, like an ocean completely filled with the nectar of realized bliss, can neither be described by speech nor conceived by mind, but can be enjoyed. Just as a hailstone falling into the sea becomes dissolved therein, so my mind becomes merged (even) in the least part of this (*parabrahman*). Now am I happy with spiritual bliss.

484. Where is this world gone? By whom was it carried away? When did it disappear? A great wonder! That which was perceived but now exists no longer.

486. Here (in the state) I neither see, nor hear, nor know anything. I am different from every other thing—the atman who is true bliss.

487. I bow before thee, O guru, who art good, great, free from attachment, the embodiment of eternal, non-dual bliss: lord of the earth, the boundless reservoir of compassion.

489. By thy grace I am happy and have attained my object, I

am freed from the shark of changing existence, and have gained the state of eternal bliss and am perfect.

490. I am without attachment and without limbs. I am sexless and indestructible. I am calm and endless. I am without stain and ancient.

491. I am not the doer, nor am I the enjoyer, I am without change and without action. I am pure intelligence, one, and eternal bliss.

493. I am neither this nor that; but I shine forth in both of them and am pure and supreme. I am neither within nor without, but I am all-pervading and non-dual Brahman.

501. I have no more connection with the body than the sky with a cloud. Whence, then, can I be subject to states (states of the body) such as waking, dreaming and dreamless slumber?

513. I am that Brahman which is like space, subtle, non-dual, without beginning and without end, and in which the whole universe, from the unmanifested down to gross matter, is known to be a mere phantom.

517. I am all-pervading; I am everything and transcend everything; I am non-dual, indestructible knowledge and eternal bliss.

518. O Guru, this supremacy over earth and heaven is attained by me through thy compassion and greatly esteemed favour. To thee, great-souled one (*Mahatma*), I bow down again and again.

519. O Guru, having in thy great compassion awakened me from the sound sleep (of ignorance), thou hast saved me, roaming about in the dream-like forest of birth, old age and death, created by *maya*, daily tormented by manifold afflictions, and terrified by the tiger of egoism.

520. O Guru, I bow down before thee who art truth alone, who hast the spendour of wisdom and who shinest in the form of the universe.

THE END

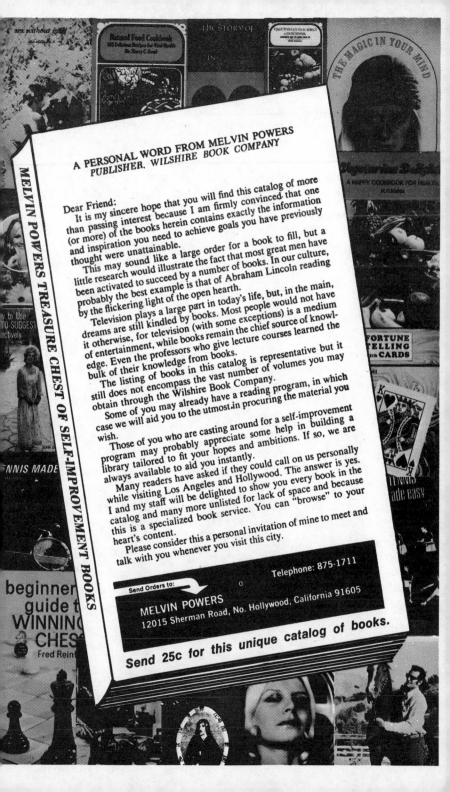

Melvin Powers
SELF-IMPROVEMENT
LIBRARY

ASTROLOGY

ASTROLOGY: A FASCINATING HISTORY *P. Naylor*	2.00
ASTROLOGY: HOW TO CHART YOUR HOROSCOPE *Max Heindel*	2.00
ASTROLOGY: YOUR PERSONAL SUN-SIGN GUIDE *Beatrice Ryder*	3.00
ASTROLOGY FOR EVERYDAY LIVING *Janet Harris*	2.00
ASTROLOGY MADE EASY *Astarte*	2.00
ASTROLOGY MADE PRACTICAL *Alexandra Kayhle*	2.00
ASTROLOGY, ROMANCE, YOU AND THE STARS *Anthony Norvell*	3.00
MY WORLD OF ASTROLOGY *Sydney Omarr*	3.00
THOUGHT DIAL *Sydney Omarr*	2.00
ZODIAC REVEALED *Rupert Gleadow*	2.00

BRIDGE, POKER & GAMBLING

ADVANCED POKER STRATEGY & WINNING PLAY *A. D. Livingston*	2.00
BRIDGE BIDDING MADE EASY *Edwin Kantar*	5.00
BRIDGE CONVENTIONS *Edwin Kantar*	4.00
COMPLETE DEFENSIVE BRIDGE PLAY *Edwin B. Kantar*	10.00
HOW TO IMPROVE YOUR BRIDGE *Alfred Sheinwold*	2.00
HOW TO WIN AT DICE GAMES *Skip Frey*	2.00
HOW TO WIN AT POKER *Terence Reese & Anthony T. Watkins*	2.00
INTRODUCTION TO DEFENDER'S PLAY *Edwin B. Kantar*	3.00
SECRETS OF WINNING POKER *George S. Coffin*	3.00
TEST YOUR BRIDGE PLAY *Edwin B. Kantar*	3.00

BUSINESS STUDY & REFERENCE

CONVERSATION MADE EASY *Elliot Russell*	2.00
EXAM SECRET *Dennis B. Jackson*	2.00
FIX-IT BOOK *Arthur Symons*	2.00
HOW TO DEVELOP A BETTER SPEAKING VOICE *M. Hellier*	2.00
HOW TO MAKE A FORTUNE IN REAL ESTATE *Albert Winnikoff*	3.00
HOW TO MAKE MONEY IN REAL ESTATE *Stanley L. McMichael*	2.00
INCREASE YOUR LEARNING POWER *Geoffrey A. Dudley*	2.00
MAGIC OF NUMBERS *Robert Tocquet*	2.00
PRACTICAL GUIDE TO BETTER CONCENTRATION *Melvin Powers*	2.00
PRACTICAL GUIDE TO PUBLIC SPEAKING *Maurice Forley*	2.00
7 DAYS TO FASTER READING *William S. Schaill*	2.00
SONGWRITERS' RHYMING DICTIONARY *Jane Shaw Whitfield*	3.00
SPELLING MADE EASY *Lester D. Basch & Dr. Milton Finkelstein*	2.00
STUDENT'S GUIDE TO BETTER GRADES *J. A. Rickard*	2.00
TEST YOURSELF — Find Your Hidden Talent *Jack Shafer*	2.00
YOUR WILL & WHAT TO DO ABOUT IT *Attorney Samuel G. Kling*	2.00

CHESS & CHECKERS

BEGINNER'S GUIDE TO WINNING CHESS *Fred Reinfeld*	2.00
BETTER CHESS — How to Play *Fred Reinfeld*	2.00
CHECKERS MADE EASY *Tom Wiswell*	2.00
CHESS IN TEN EASY LESSONS *Larry Evans*	2.00
CHESS MADE EASY *Milton L. Hanauer*	2.00
CHESS MASTERY — A New Approach *Fred Reinfeld*	2.00

_____CHESS PROBLEMS FOR BEGINNERS *edited by Fred Reinfeld* 2.0●
_____CHESS SECRETS REVEALED *Fred Reinfeld* 2.0●
_____CHESS STRATEGY — An Expert's Guide *Fred Reinfeld* 2.0●
_____CHESS TACTICS FOR BEGINNERS *edited by Fred Reinfeld* 2.0●
_____CHESS THEORY & PRACTICE *Morry & Mitchell* 2.0●
_____HOW TO WIN AT CHECKERS *Fred Reinfeld* 2.0●
_____1001 BRILLIANT WAYS TO CHECKMATE *Fred Reinfeld* 2.0●
_____1001 WINNING CHESS SACRIFICES & COMBINATIONS *Fred Reinfeld* 3.0●
_____SOVIET CHESS *Edited by R. G. Wade* 3.0●

COOKERY & HERBS

_____CULPEPER'S HERBAL REMEDIES *Dr. Nicholas Culpeper* 2.0●
_____FAST GOURMET COOKBOOK *Poppy Cannon* 2.5●
_____HEALING POWER OF HERBS *May Bethel* 2.0●
_____HERB HANDBOOK *Dawn MacLeod* 2.0●
_____HERBS FOR COOKING AND HEALING *Dr. Donald Law* 2.0●
_____HERBS FOR HEALTH How to Grow & Use Them *Louise Evans Doole* 2.0●
_____HOME GARDEN COOKBOOK Delicious Natural Food Recipes *Ken Kraft* 3.0●
_____MEDICAL HERBALIST *edited by Dr. J. R. Yemm* 3.0●
_____NATURAL FOOD COOKBOOK *Dr. Harry C. Bond* 3.0●
_____NATURE'S MEDICINES *Richard Lucas* 2.0●
_____VEGETABLE GARDENING FOR BEGINNERS *Hugh Wiberg* 2.0●
_____VEGETABLES FOR TODAY'S GARDENS *R. Milton Carleton* 2.0●
_____VEGETARIAN COOKERY *Janet Walker* 2.0●
_____VEGETARIAN COOKING MADE EASY & DELECTABLE *Veronica Vezza* 2.0●
_____VEGETARIAN DELIGHTS — A Happy Cookbook for Health *K. R. Mehta* 2.0●
_____VEGETARIAN GOURMET COOKBOOK *Joyce McKinnel* 2.0●

HEALTH

_____DR. LINDNER'S SPECIAL WEIGHT CONTROL METHOD 1.0●
_____HELP YOURSELF TO BETTER SIGHT *Margaret Darst Corbett* 3.0●
_____HOW TO IMPROVE YOUR VISION *Dr. Robert A. Kraskin* 2.0●
_____HOW YOU CAN STOP SMOKING PERMANENTLY *Ernest Caldwell* 2.0●
_____LSD — THE AGE OF MIND *Bernard Roseman* 2.0●
_____MIND OVER PLATTER *Peter G. Lindner, M.D.* 2.0●
_____NEW CARBOHYDRATE DIET COUNTER *Patti Lopez-Pereira* 1.0●
_____PSYCHEDELIC ECSTASY *William Marshall & Gilbert W. Taylor* 2.0●
_____YOU CAN LEARN TO RELAX *Dr. Samuel Gutwirth* 2.0●
_____YOUR ALLERGY—What To Do About It *Allan Knight, M.D.* 2.0●

HOBBIES

_____BATON TWIRLING — A Complete Illustrated Guide *Doris Wheelus* 4.0●
_____BEACHCOMBING FOR BEGINNERS *Norman Hickin* 2.0●
_____BLACKSTONE'S MODERN CARD TRICKS *Harry Blackstone* 2.0●
_____BLACKSTONE'S SECRETS OF MAGIC *Harry Blackstone* 2.0●
_____COIN COLLECTING FOR BEGINNERS *Burton Hobson & Fred Reinfeld* 2.0●
_____ENTERTAINING WITH ESP *Tony 'Doc' Shiels* 2.0●
_____400 FASCINATING MAGIC TRICKS YOU CAN DO *Howard Thurston* 3.0●
_____GOULD'S GOLD & SILVER GUIDE TO COINS *Maurice Gould* 2.0●
_____HOW I TURN JUNK INTO FUN AND PROFIT *Sari* 3.0●
_____HOW TO WRITE A HIT SONG & SELL IT *Tommy Boyce* 7.0●
_____JUGGLING MADE EASY *Rudolf Dittrich* 2.0●
_____MAGIC MADE EASY *Byron Wels* 2.0●
_____SEW SIMPLY, SEW RIGHT *Mini Rhea & F. Leighton* 2.0●
_____STAMP COLLECTING FOR BEGINNERS *Burton Hobson* 2.0●
_____STAMP COLLECTING FOR FUN & PROFIT *Frank Cetin* 2.0●

HORSE PLAYERS' WINNING GUIDES

_____BETTING HORSES TO WIN *Les Conklin* 2.0●
_____ELIMINATE THE LOSERS *Bob McKnight* 2.0●
_____HOW TO PICK WINNING HORSES *Bob McKnight* 2.0●
_____HOW TO WIN AT THE RACES *Sam (The Genius) Lewin* 2.0●
_____HOW YOU CAN BEAT THE RACES *Jack Kavanagh* 2.0●

____MAKING MONEY AT THE RACES *David Barr*	2.00
____PAYDAY AT THE RACES *Les Conklin*	2.00
____SMART HANDICAPPING MADE EASY *William Bauman*	2.00
____SUCCESS AT THE HARNESS RACES *Barry Meadow*	2.50

HUMOR

____BILL BALLANCE HANDBOOK OF NIFTY MOVES *Bill Ballance*	3.00
____HOW TO BE A COMEDIAN FOR FUN & PROFIT *King & Laufer*	2.00
____JOKE TELLER'S HANDBOOK *Bob Orben*	2.00

HYPNOTISM

____ADVANCED TECHNIQUES OF HYPNOSIS *Melvin Powers*	2.00
____CHILDBIRTH WITH HYPNOSIS *William S. Kroger, M.D.*	2.00
____HOW TO SOLVE YOUR SEX PROBLEMS	
WITH SELF-HYPNOSIS *Frank S. Caprio, M.D.*	2.00
____HOW TO STOP SMOKING THRU SELF-HYPNOSIS *Leslie M. LeCron*	2.00
____HOW TO USE AUTO-SUGGESTION EFFECTIVELY *John Duckworth*	2.00
____HOW YOU CAN BOWL BETTER USING SELF-HYPNOSIS *Jack Heise*	2.00
____HOW YOU CAN PLAY BETTER GOLF USING SELF-HYPNOSIS *Heise*	2.00
____HYPNOSIS AND SELF-HYPNOSIS *Bernard Hollander, M.D.*	2.00
____HYPNOTISM *(Originally published in 1893)* *Carl Sextus*	3.00
____HYPNOTISM & PSYCHIC PHENOMENA *Simeon Edmunds*	3.00
____HYPNOTISM MADE EASY *Dr. Ralph Winn*	2.00
____HYPNOTISM MADE PRACTICAL *Louis Orton*	2.00
____HYPNOTISM REVEALED *Melvin Powers*	1.00
____HYPNOTISM TODAY *Leslie LeCron & Jean Bordeaux, Ph.D.*	2.00
____MODERN HYPNOSIS *Lesley Kuhn & Salvatore Russo, Ph.D.*	3.00
____NEW CONCEPTS OF HYPNOSIS *Bernard C. Gindes, M.D.*	3.00
____POST-HYPNOTIC INSTRUCTIONS *Arnold Furst*	2.00
How to give post-hypnotic suggestions for therapeutic purposes.	
____PRACTICAL GUIDE TO SELF-HYPNOSIS *Melvin Powers*	2.00
____PRACTICAL HYPNOTISM *Philip Magonet, M.D.*	2.00
____SECRETS OF HYPNOTISM *S. J. Van Pelt, M.D.*	3.00
____SELF-HYPNOSIS *Paul Adams*	2.00
____SELF-HYPNOSIS Its Theory, Technique & Application *Melvin Powers*	2.00
____SELF-HYPNOSIS A Conditioned-Response Technique *Laurance Sparks*	3.00
____THERAPY THROUGH HYPNOSIS *edited by Raphael H. Rhodes*	3.00

JUDAICA

____HOW TO LIVE A RICHER & FULLER LIFE *Rabbi Edgar F. Magnin*	2.00
____MODERN ISRAEL *Lily Edelman*	2.00
____OUR JEWISH HERITAGE *Rabbi Alfred Wolf & Joseph Gaer*	2.00
____ROMANCE OF HASSIDISM *Jacob S. Minkin*	2.50
____SERVICE OF THE HEART *Evelyn Garfield, Ph.D.*	3.00
____STORY OF ISRAEL IN COINS *Jean & Maurice Gould*	2.00
____STORY OF ISRAEL IN STAMPS *Maxim & Gabriel Shamir*	1.00
____TONGUE OF THE PROPHETS *Robert St. John*	3.00
____TREASURY OF COMFORT *edited by Rabbi Sidney Greenberg*	3.00

MARRIAGE, SEX & PARENTHOOD

____ABILITY TO LOVE *Dr. Allan Fromme*	3.00
____ENCYCLOPEDIA OF MODERN SEX & LOVE TECHNIQUES *Macandrew*	3.00
____GUIDE TO SUCCESSFUL MARRIAGE *Drs. Albert Ellis & Robert Harper*	3.00
____HOW TO RAISE AN EMOTIONALLY HEALTHY, HAPPY CHILD, *A. Ellis*	2.00
____IMPOTENCE & FRIGIDITY *Edwin W. Hirsch, M.D.*	3.00
____JUST FOR WOMEN — A Guide to the Female Body *Richard E. Sand, M.D.*	3.00
____NEW APPROACHES TO SEX IN MARRIAGE *John E. Eichenlaub, M.D.*	3.00
____SEX WITHOUT GUILT *Albert Ellis, Ph.D.*	2.00
____SEXUALLY ADEQUATE FEMALE *Frank S. Caprio, M.D.*	2.00
____SEXUALLY ADEQUATE MALE *Frank S. Caprio, M.D.*	2.00
____YOUR FIRST YEAR OF MARRIAGE *Dr. Tom McGinnis*	2.00

METAPHYSICS & OCCULT

_____BOOK OF TALISMANS, AMULETS & ZODIACAL GEMS *William Pavitt* 3.0
_____CONCENTRATION—A Guide to Mental Mastery *Mouni Sadhu* 3.0
_____DREAMS & OMENS REVEALED *Fred Gettings* 2.0
_____EXTRASENSORY PERCEPTION *Simeon Edmunds* 2.0
_____FORTUNE TELLING WITH CARDS *P. Foli* 2.0
_____HANDWRITING ANALYSIS MADE EASY *John Marley* 2.0
_____HANDWRITING TELLS *Nadya Olyanova* 3.0
_____HOW TO UNDERSTAND YOUR DREAMS *Geoffrey A. Dudley* 2.0
_____ILLUSTRATED YOGA *William Zorn* 2.0
_____IN DAYS OF GREAT PEACE *Mouni Sadhu* 3.0
_____KING SOLOMON'S TEMPLE IN THE MASONIC TRADITION *Alex Horne* 5.0
_____MAGICIAN — His training and work *W. E. Butler* 2.0
_____MEDITATION *Mouni Sadhu* 3.0
_____MODERN NUMEROLOGY *Morris C. Goodman* 2.0
_____NUMEROLOGY—ITS FACTS AND SECRETS *Ariel Yvon Taylor* 2.0
_____PALMISTRY MADE EASY *Fred Gettings* 2.0
_____PALMISTRY MADE PRACTICAL *Elizabeth Daniels Squire* 3.0
_____PALMISTRY SECRETS REVEALED *Henry Frith* 2.0
_____PRACTICAL YOGA *Ernest Wood* 3.0
_____PROPHECY IN OUR TIME *Martin Ebon* 2.5
_____PSYCHOLOGY OF HANDWRITING *Nadya Olyanova* 2.0
_____SEEING INTO THE FUTURE *Harvey Day* 2.0
_____SUPERSTITION — Are you superstitious? *Eric Maple* 2.0
_____TAROT *Mouni Sadhu* 4.0
_____TAROT OF THE BOHEMIANS *Papus* 3.0
_____TEST YOUR ESP *Martin Ebon* 2.0
_____WAYS TO SELF-REALIZATION *Mouni Sadhu* 2.0
_____WITCHCRAFT, MAGIC & OCCULTISM—A Fascinating History *W. B. Crow* 3.0
_____WITCHCRAFT — THE SIXTH SENSE *Justine Glass* 2.0
_____WORLD OF PSYCHIC RESEARCH *Hereward Carrington* 2.0
_____YOU CAN ANALYZE HANDWRITING *Robert Holder* 2.0

SELF-HELP & INSPIRATIONAL

_____CYBERNETICS WITHIN US *Y. Saparina* 3.0
_____DAILY POWER FOR JOYFUL LIVING *Dr. Donald Curtis* 2.0
_____DOCTOR PSYCHO-CYBERNETICS *Maxwell Maltz, M.D.* 3.0
_____DYNAMIC THINKING *Melvin Powers* 1.0
_____GREATEST POWER IN THE UNIVERSE *U. S. Andersen* 4.0
_____GROW RICH WHILE YOU SLEEP *Ben Sweetland* 2.0
_____GROWTH THROUGH REASON *Albert Ellis, Ph.D.* 3.0
_____GUIDE TO DEVELOPING YOUR POTENTIAL *Herbert A. Otto, Ph.D.* 3.0
_____GUIDE TO LIVING IN BALANCE *Frank S. Caprio, M.D.* 2.0
_____HELPING YOURSELF WITH APPLIED PSYCHOLOGY *R. Henderson* 2.0
_____HELPING YOURSELF WITH PSYCHIATRY *Frank S. Caprio, M.D.* 2
_____HOW TO ATTRACT GOOD LUCK *A. H. Z. Carr* 2.0
_____HOW TO CONTROL YOUR DESTINY *Norvell* 2.0
_____HOW TO DEVELOP A WINNING PERSONALITY *Martin Panzer* 3.0
_____HOW TO DEVELOP AN EXCEPTIONAL MEMORY *Young & Gibson* 3.0
_____HOW TO OVERCOME YOUR FEARS *M. P. Leahy, M.D.* 2.0
_____HOW YOU CAN HAVE CONFIDENCE AND POWER *Les Giblin* 2.0
_____HUMAN PROBLEMS & HOW TO SOLVE THEM *Dr. Donald Curtis* 2.0
_____I CAN *Ben Sweetland* 3.0
_____I WILL *Ben Sweetland* 2.0
_____LEFT-HANDED PEOPLE *Michael Barsley* 3.0
_____MAGIC IN YOUR MIND *U. S. Andersen* 3.0
_____MAGIC OF THINKING BIG *Dr. David J. Schwartz* 2.0
_____MAGIC POWER OF YOUR MIND *Walter M. Germain* 3.0
_____MENTAL POWER THRU SLEEP SUGGESTION *Melvin Powers* 1.0
_____NEW GUIDE TO RATIONAL LIVING *Albert Ellis, Ph.D. - R. Harper, Ph.D.* 3
_____ORIENTAL SECRETS OF GRACEFUL LIVING *Boye De Mente* 1.0
_____OUR TROUBLED SELVES *Dr. Allan Fromme* 3

*The books listed above can be obtained from your book dealer or directly from
Melvin Powers. When ordering, please remit 25c per book postage & handling.
Send 25c for our illustrated catalog of self-improvement books.*

Melvin Powers

12015 Sherman Road, No. Hollywood, California 91605

WILSHIRE HORSE LOVERS' LIBRARY

AMATEUR HORSE BREEDER A. C. Leighton Hardman	2.00
AMERICAN QUARTER HORSE IN PICTURES Margaret Cabell Self	2.00
APPALOOSA HORSE Bill & Dona Richardson	2.00
ARABIAN HORSE Reginald S. Summerhays	2.00
ART OF WESTERN RIDING Suzanne Norton Jones	2.00
AT THE HORSE SHOW Margaret Cabell Self	2.00
BACK-YARD FOAL Peggy Jett Pittinger	2.00
BACK-YARD HORSE Peggy Jett Pittinger	2.00
BASIC DRESSAGE Jean Froissard	2.00
BEGINNER'S GUIDE TO HORSEBACK RIDING Sheila Wall	2.00
BEGINNER'S GUIDE TO THE WESTERN HORSE Natlee Kenoyer	2.00
BITS—THEIR HISTORY, USE AND MISUSE Louis Taylor	2.00
BREAKING & TRAINING THE DRIVING HORSE Doris Ganton	2.00
CAVALRY MANUAL OF HORSEMANSHIP Gordon Wright	3.00
COMPLETE TRAINING OF HORSE AND RIDER Colonel Alois Podhajsky	3.00
DISORDERS OF THE HORSE & WHAT TO DO ABOUT THEM E. Hanauer	2.00
DOG TRAINING MADE EASY & FUN John W. Kellogg	2.00
DRESSAGE—A study of the Finer Points in Riding Henry Wynmalen	3.00
DRIVING HORSES Sallie Walrond	2.00
ENDURANCE RIDING Ann Hyland	2.00
EQUITATION Jean Froissard	3.00
FIRST AID FOR HORSES Dr. Charles H. Denning, Jr.	2.00
FUN OF RAISING A COLT Rubye & Frank Griffith	2.00
FUN ON HORSEBACK Margaret Cabell Self	3.00
HORSE DISEASES—Causes, Symptoms & Treatment Dr. H. G. Belschner	3.00
HORSE OWNER'S CONCISE GUIDE Elsie V. Hanauer	2.00
HORSE SELECTION & CARE FOR BEGINNERS George H. Conn	3.00
HORSE SENSE—A complete guide to riding and care Alan Deacon	4.00
HORSEBACK RIDING FOR BEGINNERS Louis Taylor	3.00
HORSEBACK RIDING MADE EASY & FUN Sue Henderson Coen	3.00
HORSES—Their Selection, Care & Handling Margaret Cabell Self	2.00
HOW TO BUY A BETTER HORSE & SELL THE HORSE YOU OWN	3.00
HOW TO ENJOY YOUR QUARTER HORSE Williard H. Porter	2.00
HUNTER IN PICTURES Margaret Cabell Self	2.00
ILLUSTRATED BOOK OF THE HORSE S. Sidney (8½″ x 11½″)	10.00
ILLUSTRATED HORSE MANAGEMENT—400 Illustrations Dr. E. Mayhew	5.00
ILLUSTRATED HORSE TRAINING Captain M. H. Hayes	5.00
ILLUSTRATED HORSEBACK RIDING FOR BEGINNERS Jeanne Mellin	2.00
JUMPING—Learning and Teaching Jean Froissard	2.00
KNOW ALL ABOUT HORSES Harry Disston	2.00
LAME HORSE—Causes, Symptoms & Treatment Dr. James R. Rooney	3.00
LAW & YOUR HORSE Edward H. Greene	3.00
LIPIZZANERS & THE SPANISH RIDING SCHOOL W. Reuter (4¼″ x 6″)	2.50
MORGAN HORSE IN PICTURES Margaret Cabell Self	2.00
MOVIE HORSES—The Fascinating Techniques of Training Anthony Amaral	2.00
POLICE HORSES Judith Campbell	2.00
PRACTICAL GUIDE TO HORSESHOEING	2.00
PRACTICAL GUIDE TO OWNING YOUR OWN HORSE Steven D. Price	2.00
PRACTICAL HORSE PSYCHOLOGY Moyra Williams	2.00
PROBLEM HORSES Guide for Curing Serious Behavior Habits Summerhays	2.00
RESCHOOLING THE THOROUGHBRED Peggy Jett Pittenger	2.00
RIDE WESTERN Louis Taylor	2.00
SCHOOLING YOUR YOUNG HORSE George Wheatley	2.00
STABLE MANAGEMENT FOR THE OWNER-GROOM George Wheatley	3.00
STALLION MANAGEMENT—A Guide for Stud Owners A. C. Hardman	2.00
TEACHING YOUR HORSE TO JUMP W. J. Froud	2.00
TRAIL HORSES & TRAIL RIDING Anne & Perry Westbrook	2.00
TREATING COMMON DISEASES OF YOUR HORSE Dr. George H. Conn	2.00
TREATING HORSE AILMENTS G. W. Serth	2.00
WESTERN HORSEBACK RIDING Glen Balch	2.00
WONDERFUL WORLD OF PONIES Peggy Jett Pittenger (8½″ x 11½″)	4.00
YOUR FIRST HORSE George C. Saunders, M.D.	2.00
YOUR PONY BOOK Hermann Wiederhold	2.00
YOUR WESTERN HORSE Nelson C. Nye	2.00

The books listed above can be obtained from your book dealer or directly from Melvin Powers. When ordering, please remit 25c per book postage & handling.
Send 25c for our illustrated catalog of self-improvement books.
Melvin Powers, 12015 Sherman Road, No. Hollywood, California 91605